It might just happen to work

It might just happen to work

Billy Williamson

The Shetland Times Ltd
Lerwick
2023

It might just happen to work

First published by The Shetland Times, 2023.

ISBN 978-1-910997-55-0

Sketches by Kari Williamson.

A catalogue record for this book is available from the British Library.
British Library Cataloguing-in-Publication Data

Printed and Published by
The Shetland Times Ltd.,
Gremista, Lerwick,
Shetland ZE1 0PX.

Preface

My father, Willie Williamson (Jnr), was born in 1903 in West Yell in the Shetland Isles. He had an early misfortune in contracting polio, which left him with a slight limp and a permanent weakness in his right leg. Nevertheless, he was something of a mechanical prodigy and became very interested in modern inventions, such as the gramophone, radio, photography and the developing arrival of motor-powered vehicles in Shetland. He studied the latest news about new developments and made experiments with radio and photography, as well as bicycles and all other means of transport, and eventually became one of Shetland's earliest motorists.

In later years he frequently entertained his family and friends with interesting and amusing tales from these pioneering days. His family were keen that he should write down these stories with the aim of preserving and perhaps publishing them. Sadly he never got around to it, although he did make notes of some of the content he intended to use. These still exist and, using them and family memories, I thought it might be possible to produce a fairly accurate copy of the book he hoped to produce and this publication is the result.

For the sake of variety I have also included some other interesting or amusing stories from the same period. The sketches included in this book are by my late sister Kari, who is mentioned through the text.

Billy Williamson

2023

It Might Just Happen to Work

One of Willie's uncles, John Sinclair, built an induction coil and used it to treat his damaged leg. Whether or not this helped is uncertain, but it was a fashionable treatment at that time. It certainly did exercise the muscles so it is quite possible that it may have helped to a certain extent.

Willie did not give in easily to his disability and tried as far as possible to lead a 'normal' boy's life. One day, with his brother George – the one nearest to him in age – they met an elderly woman who spoke to them, as people did in those days. In the course of their conversation she remarked that because of her age she would not be around much longer. George considered this too pessimistic and replied, "Well, you never know your luck."

Willie recovered enough to go to school but I don't think he ever enjoyed it much. Despite the saying, which you still hear today, that school days are the happiest days of your life – but which I suspect they rarely are – in Willie's case they certainly were not. I think the same was true of his older brother Henry, who later admitted that he left school on his birthday, as soon as he could legally do so; he did not wait until the end of term or even the end of the week.

It was a one-teacher school and, although the teacher was Willie's aunt-in-law (whose husband had built the induction coil used on his leg), he always thought that she disliked him and would pick on him to use as a scapegoat whenever any mischief took place. On one occasion she spent considerable time trying to work out how one of the more favoured pupils had managed to get the right answer to a sum when he not done it correctly. Willie's opinion was, "If it had been me, it would not have taken her long to work it out."

Nor was he very impressed with his first school prize-book. It was called *Johnnie's Work* and told the story of an apprentice undertaker.

He was much happier with the one he was given by his strict and highly religious grandmother, Anderina: *Highwaymen and Robbers* told of nefarious goings on in the olden days.

Of course, in those days and for many years later, schoolchildren were often treated in ways that would be quite unacceptable today. There were, however, some amusing incidents – often unintentional – such as the one that happened at a school concert when two boys were to act out a moral tale. They were portraying boys who met on a Sunday morning: one, the hero representing good, was on his way to church; the other, as the villain, was going fishing. The hero tried to show the other the error of his ways, and eventually succeeded. Here, the reformed sinner was supposed to show his conversion by breaking his fishing rod over his knee. At this point, however, it all went wrong. Instead of the rod breaking in two as was intended, it broke into three pieces and the centre section shot out and hit the hero on the nose. Whether or not this detracted from the moral message we will never know, but it certainly amused the assembled children and there seems little doubt that they would have voted it the best act of the concert.

Motorcycle Stories

After leaving school there were, of course, very few jobs available. Willie thought of trying to get work on a local fishing boat, but his father, William James Williamson (Willie Snr), was very much against this. This kind of fishing is, and always has been, a dangerous way to make a living. Even today it remains one of the most accident-prone of all professions, even when practised by well-trained and able-bodied people. Willie Snr probably thought, quite correctly, that Willie's disability made him unsuited to this kind of work.

If Willie Jnr retained any thoughts of a seafaring career, they vanished when he discovered that he was susceptible to sea-sickness. Older seamen assured him that he would soon get over it, but he did not think that he could put up with it long enough for this to happen. Anyone who has experienced this most miserable of complaints will be deeply sympathetic to this point of view.

Willie's strength had improved to the extent that he thought he would be able to ride a motorcycle and he started the difficult task of saving enough to afford to buy one. Having abandoned the fishing boat idea, about the only paid work available to him – as to most young men of the period – was as a day labourer, on the croft, or in the work of cutting, curing and transporting peats by wheelbarrow or horse and cart, so saving was a slow, laborious business.

But eventually the great day came and he took delivery of his first motorcycle: a 1910 Douglas, single speed. The only way to start it was by running along with it and jumping into the saddle when it started. How he managed to ride it at all, with the slight limp and permanent weakness in his right leg caused by his boyhood polio, is something of a mystery.

Nevertheless, Willie seemed to manage his bike reasonably well and drove all over Yell, despite its notoriously bad roads, carrying goods from shops, or even pillion passengers. Only once did he have a slight mishap, when his trouser leg became entangled in the footrest, causing a minor accident. Fortunately the only damage was to his trousers.

Over the next few years Willie upgraded his cycles by exchanging them for more modern types, though he still remained faithful to the Douglas marque. He was a fan of the horizontally-opposed twin cylinder engine which Douglas used for many years. It is indeed a very smooth-running type, though sometimes troubled with overheating caused by uneven airflow over the two cylinders. First came a 1916 model, 2-speed, belt-driven with lights, probably acetylene, but still no clutch. Next a 1921 model, more powerful at 4hp. Then a 1927 with clutch, kick-starter and chain drive. It had no lights but Willie fitted them. They were probably electric. However, even with the kick-starter he could not start the engine in the normal way by standing astride the machine facing forward and pushing down the starter pedal with the right foot. The polio had weakened his right leg too much for this to be possible so, instead, he had to stand at the right side of the bike and use his left foot on the kick-starter. He did not seem to have any trouble doing this. He then rebuilt a 1929 model using parts from more than one cycle.

Meanwhile, George had also taken up motorcycling. Unlike Willie, he seems to have used a variety of different makes in succession –

Motosacoche, Douglas, Jap, New Imperial, BSA, Royal Enfield – finishing up with a Lambretta scooter. One of his first was a Levis which, before electric lighting had become almost universal for motorcycles, used acetylene gas to power the lights. One winter night when he was driving over a very rough piece of road the headlamp went out, leaving him in darkness. He had to stop and investigate but unfortunately set his right foot in the drain, causing him to fall over and bring the bike on top of him. It turned out that the gas pipe supplying the headlamp had somehow become jammed between the coils of the front fork springs, but he was soon able to fix it and continue on his way.

At about the same time, Charlie Nicholson of North-a-Voe had acquired a P & M motorbike with sidecar (which may have belonged to the late Dr Taylor). George became interested in this version of the motorcycle and arranged to have a trial run with it. His first attempt was, perhaps, not well advised as he decided to drive down what was called the 'Kings Road'. The origin of the name is obscure. Someone told me that every district had a Kings Road but I have never been able to ascertain if this is so. I certainly never encountered another one. I think, however, that it is unlikely His Majesty George V (I think it would have been him at that time) ever spent much time there. The road is very steep and coming down it meant George (Williamson, not His Majesty) had to negotiate a right-angle turn at the bottom, where a house called the Smiddy is situated just at the corner. Changing over from driving single bikes to bikes with sidecars is not easy. In this case it was made even worse by the fact that, as George realised half-way down, this sidecar was mounted on the right-hand side of the bike, not the more usual left, and when he tried to turn right into the district called Seafield the sidecar lifted clear off the road. To get it back to normal he had to turn back in the opposite direction, ending up in the drain at the back of the Smiddy. By great good luck neither George nor the bike suffered any serious damage.

The trouble with changing from driving a single to driving a combination is caused by the built-in computer that we all possess. When driving a two-wheeled vehicle it is continually making small steering adjustments to maintain the machine's balance. With three wheels this is not needed, but our computer does not understand this and persists in making them, which is more of a hindrance than a help. Eventually the computer manages to re-programme itself to suit the new situation, but it does take time.

Some drivers favoured the combination with a sidecar attached. The oldest Williamson brother, John (usually called Donny), was particularly fond of this type of machine, an attraction being that his wife Matty, who was quite a large woman, found the padded seating much more comfortable than having to perch on the pillion.

George had another mishap when he was riding a Douglas motorcycle, of the same model as the one used by Willie, which could only be started by pushing it then jumping into the saddle when it got going. While he was still running alongside trying to keep it going, his trouser leg somehow got caught in the footrest and split up to his knee. He managed to keep running, with trouser leg flapping in the breeze, but he could not reach the throttle further along the handlebars to stop the bike, so it kept going faster and faster. When he could no longer keep up with it he had to let go and the bike ended up in the drain. The situation was not helped by the passenger he had taken with him who could not resist the temptation to roar with laughter. Undeterred, he made a second attempt, this time with success, and completed his journey.

One time Willie lent the youngest brother, Hughie, his bike to take his girlfriend to a dance. Whether she was of unusual size I do not know, but Hughie was unsure of the bike's ability to carry their combined weight up the hills they would encounter, so he devised a solution – perhaps inspired by the tales of chivalry popular in an earlier age – and arranged it so that the lady would not have to walk at all. When they came to a hill he would jump off without stopping and, with the engine still running, would run alongside the bike, holding on to the handlebars so he was still able to control it. When they came to the top of the hill he would leap nimbly, if a little breathlessly, back into the saddle.

The lack of paid employment in the isles meant a great number of Shetland men had to spend a considerable amount of their lives at sea in order to make and save enough money to make living in the isles feasible. On returning home it was common for them to come with some luxury item which would be of use on the croft, which many were involved with.

Motorcycles fitted into this category with many machines, including all the prominent British makes, coming to Shetland in this way. Whenever a social function was held in one of the village halls a walk past would reveal a bewildering collection of motorbikes leaning along the sides of the hall.

One of these was obtained by a man called Tammy who lived with his brother (a married man with a young family). One day a passing pedestrian stopped to admire the peaceful scene: a group of young children playing outside a cottage and glancing occasionally with wonderment at the strange machine standing outside the gate. Suddenly the cottage door opened and their father stepped out. "Johnny, Charlie, Vina, come in at once, Tammy is going to try her!" There seems to be no record of a serious accident at that time so we can assume that Tammy's effort was at least partly successful.

Motorcycling had become firmly established in Shetland, particularly in Yell where the motorcycle had a remarkable reputation as the preferred mode of transport well into the 1970s. After the Second World War, when so many young men spent the British winter working as whalers at South Georgia, they would often return home with a beautiful, shiny, brand new machine. And the availability of cheap, good-quality ex-military bikes at this time increased still more the number in use – someone estimated that there were 300 in Yell alone.

At this time the motorcyclist's outfit was almost a uniform: an ex-Home Guard coat, cheesecutter cap, gauntlet gloves and rubber boots. Often they were also encumbered by paraffin flasks, wrapped-up parcels, recycled biscuit boxes, etc. Perhaps they were not all entirely satisfied with this however, as a story current at the time was of one local man who saved up very conscientiously and eventually purchased a professional motorcyclist outfit, only to discover that he then did not have enough money left to buy the motorcycle.

Of course, not everyone could afford a new bike, or if something happened to their usual bike it had to be repaired as cheaply as possible. Many riders also resorted to improvisation for temporary repairs. One man ran for years on his bike after it had developed a cracked frame. He had to sit in the saddle so that his weight would cause the frame to spread enough to allow the chain drive to engage the driving and driven gear wheels. Another found that his clutch had failed due to a faulty operating cable. As he had no spare and had an important trip to make, he tied a piece of string to the operating lever on the gearbox and recruited one of his neighbours, Johnny Mann, to sit on the pillion and follow the rider's instructions, pull, pull, pull, slip, slip slip until the trip was completed.

There were no regulations about tread depth on tyres so they were almost never replaced until they started to disintegrate, when they would either be given to children as toys or form the centrepiece of a celebration bonfire. Inflatable tyres of the time were by no means foolproof and it was not uncommon when pumping up a tyre for it to suddenly blow off the rim. On at least one occasion Willie had to resort to using a length of clothesline to tie it on and complete his journey.

Willie had taught himself to solder so was often called upon to help with minor repairs. One man became obsessed with the idea that his motorcycle fuel tank was leaking and had Willie repair leaks which were frequently not even there. His client would always insist that the tank would really need to be tested under pressure. Willie knew that this was unnecessary as it was never subjected to any pressure in normal use. Eventually, however, he became fed up with looking for dubious leaks and decided that a bit of psychology might be more successful. He assured his client that this time he had tested it under quite a high pressure and no leak had been found. His client never again reported any trouble with leaks.

Willie was sometimes called upon to give motorcycle driving lessons and one of his pupils, Andy, had difficulty in understanding the role of the clutch in starting off. Why, he wondered, not just put the gear lever directly into gear? Willie tried to explain to him that (a) it probably would not go into gear, and (b) if it did, the start would be far too abrupt. Andy was not convinced and one day during his lesson he decided to test his theory. As was his practice he left Willie to watch his progress, rode a few hundred yards down the road then stopped, turned round and prepared to start on the way back. Ignoring the clutch he pushed the gear lever into gear. By sheer luck, good or bad according to your point of view, it did go in. The cycle gave a huge jump forward, leaving Andy sitting on the road like an unhorsed knight, then ran a couple of metres and fell over on its side with petrol running out of the tank. Andy struggled to his feet and came forward to retrieve his fallen steed. He then remounted, restarted the engine, this time using the clutch, and drove back. Sometimes one practical demonstration is worth any number of theoretical lectures and I think we can be sure that Andy never again tried to dispense with the clutch.

Coincidentally, Willie was also teaching Andy to play the fiddle. It is doubtful how successful this was as on one occasion he rushed into Willie's workshop in a state of great excitement carrying his fiddle and began to play. When he finished he asked, "Do you recognise that tune?" Willie could not honestly say that he had. At this Andy added, "Do you not think it sounded a bit like ...?" and named a simple Shetland tune often played by beginners. Again, Willie could not honestly say that he had noticed any resemblance to the named tune. But it was at least a safer occupation.

A common practice in those days, which would be regarded with horror today, was carrying young children on the motorcycle fuel tank. It was actually considered safer this way than on the pillion, where a child might fall off without anyone knowing. On the tank they were at least restrained by the rider's encircling arms.

Willie's daughter Kari remembered being carried this way on many occasions. Willie always wore long gauntlet gloves when driving and she was instructed to keep a tight hold on these. Particularly memorable was the time the family set out berry picking. There is a type of heather which produces berries which, although quite small, are very tasty. So off they set – armed with jars to contain their collection and the hope of perhaps getting enough to make perhaps a pot of jam – Willie in the saddle, Kari and her mother Tamar in the sidecar, and Tamar's sister Zena on the pillion.

They had not gone very far before they were suddenly enveloped in what seemed to Kari to be a thick grey blanket, while to the adults it seemed like a scene from a science fiction film. Almost instantly it became obvious what had happened. They'd had the misfortune to encounter the curse of Shetland summers – a swarm of midges. Although some protective measures such as lotions or fine mesh nets are now available, in those days, at least, the fact was that it was just not possible to carry out any outdoor activity in those conditions so they had to return home, safe and sound but, alas, berryless.

A huge number of motorcycles were used for everyday travel in Shetland. Some of the more popular makes were: Matchless, Triumph, Norton, Ariel, BSA, Royal Enfield, Douglas, Velocette, Sunbeam, Rudge AJS, BSA, Bantam, Panther, Brough Superior, James, OK-Supreme, Vincent, Excelsior, Cotton, Levis, Francis-Barnett, Raleigh, Humber, Norman, Scott, Excelsior.

A Brush with the Law

It was in the late 1930s that Willie became innocently involved in a court case. It all started peacefully enough when an acquaintance of his came along to his workshop in North-a-Voe to ask him to have a look at his motorbike. It was obvious to Willie that the bike had run into something. Subsequent enquiries revealed that the rider had run into one of the gates which were still common on Yell's public roads. This was unfortunate as it meant that the police would almost certainly become involved.

Sure enough, a rash of summonses soon arrived at addresses in North-a-Voe and the neighbouring village of Basta. The motorcyclist was well known as being a heavy drinker, but on the day of the accident he seems to have spoken to as many people as possible and later had them called as witnesses to testify that he had been completely sober. One of those called as a witness was a woman who lived in the house of Lower Camb but, in fact, she had not seen or spoken to the driver of the motorcycle on the occasion of the incident. Eventually she managed to see him and told him that because of this she could not possibly attend as a witness. He refused to accept this. "Yes, yes, I spoke to you that night. Remember, you were on the brigstanes of Camb!"

It had, in fact, been her sister-in-law with whom he had spoken. She had decided to call along her in-laws on her way home from shopping. The motorcyclist was quite familiar with everyone in the district, including the two ladies, who were nothing alike. One of them even had a very conspicuous limp, by a curious coincidence caused by the same outbreak of polio that had caused Willie's disability. Her limp was much worse than Willie's, and therefore the motorcyclist ought to have been able to recognise at a glance which lady was which when he was in, what was known as, his 'sober senses'.

The motorcyclist had pleaded not guilty and the trial was to be held in Lerwick Sheriff Court. All those involved were to travel to Lerwick on the steamer, *Earl of Zetland*. On the day of their departure the defendant was still quite confident of being acquitted and wandered around the boat with a half-bottle of whisky, treating the witnesses.

Willie had been called to describe the unusual gearing system on this bike, which could be rather awkward to use. The proceedings got under way and, as expert witness, Willie described the problems with the gears. He was also asked if he considered that the defendant was drunk at the time at the time he saw him, just after the incident. Anyone who remembers the TV programme *Perry Mason* will remember that at this point Mason would have jumped to his feet and said, "Objection! This witness is an engineer, not a medical practitioner." Which would have been answered with, "Objection sustained."

Willie, having no such guidance and not wishing to commit himself, merely replied that he had smelt drink on his breath. Back on more familiar ground, he agreed that the gears were awkward to use. The most serious fault was that it was very easy to think that you had put the box into neutral when, in fact, it was still in a forward gear. In the worst case scenario you might then release the clutch lever, causing the machine to spring forward and hit anything in front of it.

It was just possible that the gate had been damaged in this way, but when the defendant gave his evidence he did not mention the gears at all and thereby perhaps threw away his last chance of avoiding conviction. Inevitably he was found guilty and presumably fined, and may perhaps have been ordered to pay for repairs to the gate, though I have been unable to find any information on this. For some reason he continued to blame Willie for the unfavourable verdict, and for weeks afterwards never spoke to him.

Then came the incident of the horse and cart. The defendant was probably more familiar with driving the horse and cart than the motorcycle and one day, while driving this combination, one of the cart wheels worked loose and fell off. While he was struggling with it, Willie came past and immediately came to his assistance. Between the two of them, and Willie's well-known mechanical skills, they soon had things back together and working and the driver was able to continue his journey. This broke the ice, and afterwards they always met on friendly terms although they were never likely to become close friends as Willie was a teetotaller and the cart driver was a heavy drinker. It is unlikely, either, that Willie was paid for his help. The cart driver had a favourite phrase whenever someone had done him an obligement: "Joy, I would pay you but I know you wouldn't take it."

By the way, it was not necessary to be drunk or have troublesome gears to have difficulty with gates and once one of Willie's employers knocked one down on the road to North Roe.

The First Cars

The first car in Yell, and probably one of the first in Shetland, was owned by the doctor, H.P. Taylor. In his autobiography he describes it as a single cylinder, with pull start, and of French manufacture. It seems to have been difficult to start and prone to a variety of problems. He did not have it long and replaced it several times but, in 1912, he acquired a Model T Ford. He seems to have been a rather poor driver and frequently got into trouble. He painted a red mark on a wall near his garage to remind him where to start turning the steering wheel to bring him out on the road.

The main road into North-a-Voe, known as the Camb road, included a very steep section where it joined the main north-south road and, to make matters even more difficult, had a gate across it. It was, to put it mildly, an extremely awkward position for a gate. When coming up to it, if you had no helper you had to either have great confidence in your hand brake, stop the engine and put it in gear, or carry something suitable to jam one of the wheels. Eventually Dr Taylor made himself a wooden block for this purpose. He had a rope attached to it so he could take his seat in the car and have the engine running before pulling on the rope to remove his safety device.

But it was no surprise when one day Dr Taylor slipped off the road and partially into the ditch at this point. Some people who were working nearby saw the accident and walked over to the scene. Dr Taylor was still hanging on to the steering wheel, with his foot pressing grimly as hard as possible on the brake. "Send for Willie Williamson," he shouted to them.

Willie lived not far away so someone was sent to call him. Willie duly appeared and soon had the car back on the road again. After that the doctor frequently called on Willie for help when he had mechanical problems. One of these involved fitting a spare part in a rather inaccessible place on the machine. None of Willie's tools seemed suitable, so he started to rummage through the doctor's tool box and found something that looked promising. It worked perfectly so he asked the doctor what it was for. "It was used in an appendicitis operation," the doctor said. He then presented Willie with an old set which he used for many years.

Willie also noticed a stout wooden box with 'ADT' painted boldly on it. "What does ADT stand for?" he asked.

"It stands for Any Damned Thing," he was told.

Most of us, I suspect, have at least one box which could be accurately described in this way, but few would advertise it.

Kari witnessed the incident with the doctor's car and the gate and had, at the tender age of six, decided to go into business. There was another gate nearby on the main road and when out playing she formed the habit of watching for approaching traffic. When she saw a car approaching she would run and open the gate for it, closing it after it had gone through. For this service she was usually rewarded with a handful of loose change.

Although more cars came into use in Yell, they did not suddenly replace the motorbike in the way that the motorcycle had replaced the gig. Even with the coming of the Model T, cars were still far too expensive for most people.

Donny progressed to a three-wheeler car. These looked just like an ordinary small car but could be legally driven by anyone who had only a motorcycle driving licence. A version of this car which later became very popular was the Reliant Robin, which was immune to rust as the body was made of fibreglass. Its main disadvantage was that the single front wheel made it difficult to drive in snow as it ploughed a separate single track. It was also quite light so could be difficult to handle in high winds.

At least one man had a Morgan which had two wheels in front and one behind, which was also the driving wheel. The three-wheeler gave more comfort for the driver and passenger, or allowed an extra passenger to be carried. Often, however, the standard motorcycle combination machine was used for shopping, when the sidecar was used to carry goods purchased. A bonus was that they were more convenient when a gate was encountered as they could be left standing without having to be propped up while the driver opened and closed the gate.

Nevertheless cars, especially the Model T, did begin to appear, mostly used as taxis. They were not without their faults though. They had no windscreen wipers, so a potato cut in half could be wiped over it, acting as a wetting agent and helping to disperse the raindrops. The clutch was a frequent source of trouble. If it had a tendency to slip, Fuller's earth could be applied to it as a temporary expedient. If too fierce, Codza oil could be used for a smoother action. The prudent motorist always carried a supply of both of these. In the event of a puncture, a Stepney wheel could be used to let you drive home; it simply clamped on to the side of the affected wheel. It worked reasonably well in dry weather but as it was outside the mudguard it could be very wet and messy in the rain. If the radiator became partly blocked, causing overheating, it could sometimes be cleared by pouring caustic soda into it.

The salt-laden winds made rust a constant problem, with no real solution other than scraping it off with a wire brush and covering up with paint; an eternal losing battle. If it had been feasible to carry out regular washing with fresh water to remove the salt that might have helped, but with no piped mains water supply it was really not practical to do this regularly enough to make any real difference.

No-one could afford antifreeze even if the radiator did not leak, which it usually did, so it had to be drained every night in frosty weather then filled again the next morning. Sometimes kettles of water were boiled for this as the hot water helped with the car starting.

Another long-term problem was keeping the battery charged in winter. On an island most journeys are quite short and, in these northern latitudes, daylight hours in winter are very short indeed. Finding yourself with a flat battery meant either vigorous use of the starting handle, which was very hard work, or pushing – if the road was suitable and had no awkwardly placed gradients – which was also very hard work, even if a number of people were present. Sometimes another vehicle was available which could give you a tow, but it was rare to be that lucky. As a result, drivers were tempted to use as little lighting as possible, often crawling along on side lamps only when headlamps would have been safer but were too extravagant with battery power. Some people had wind-powered chargers and after the war it was possible to buy hand-powered battery chargers, but using those was again hard work and painfully slow. When driving in the dark one had to be careful not to race the engine too much for fear of burning out the headlamp bulbs.

With the Model T and some other cars, water on the coils (or commutator) meant lying on your back under the engine to dry and clean the affected part. If difficulty in starting was a problem it was sometimes possible in a dire emergency to take the car up a hill by putting it in gear and winding it up using the starting handle, very hard and slow work, so only done when all else had failed.

Cars were very susceptible to any form of dampness and on one famous occasion the local agricultural show, held at Windhouse, was badly disrupted by torrential rain and only one of the cars attending was able to keep going. More often, however, it was just misty drizzle that caused the problem. There was little that could be done to prevent this other than trying to keep the car as dry as possible. Once it had stopped one could only clean and dry all the surfaces which were subjected to high voltages – coil, plug leads and distributor cap etc – with a dry cloth. If meth was available this could help considerably; sometimes petrol was used but this was less effective and could be dangerous as it was so flammable.

The Model T was a relatively light car so in the event of minor mishaps, such as slipping into a ditch, it could often be set back in place by manhandling by a few volunteers, though few could equal the achievements of the prominent Shetland Mainland driver known as 'Deaf

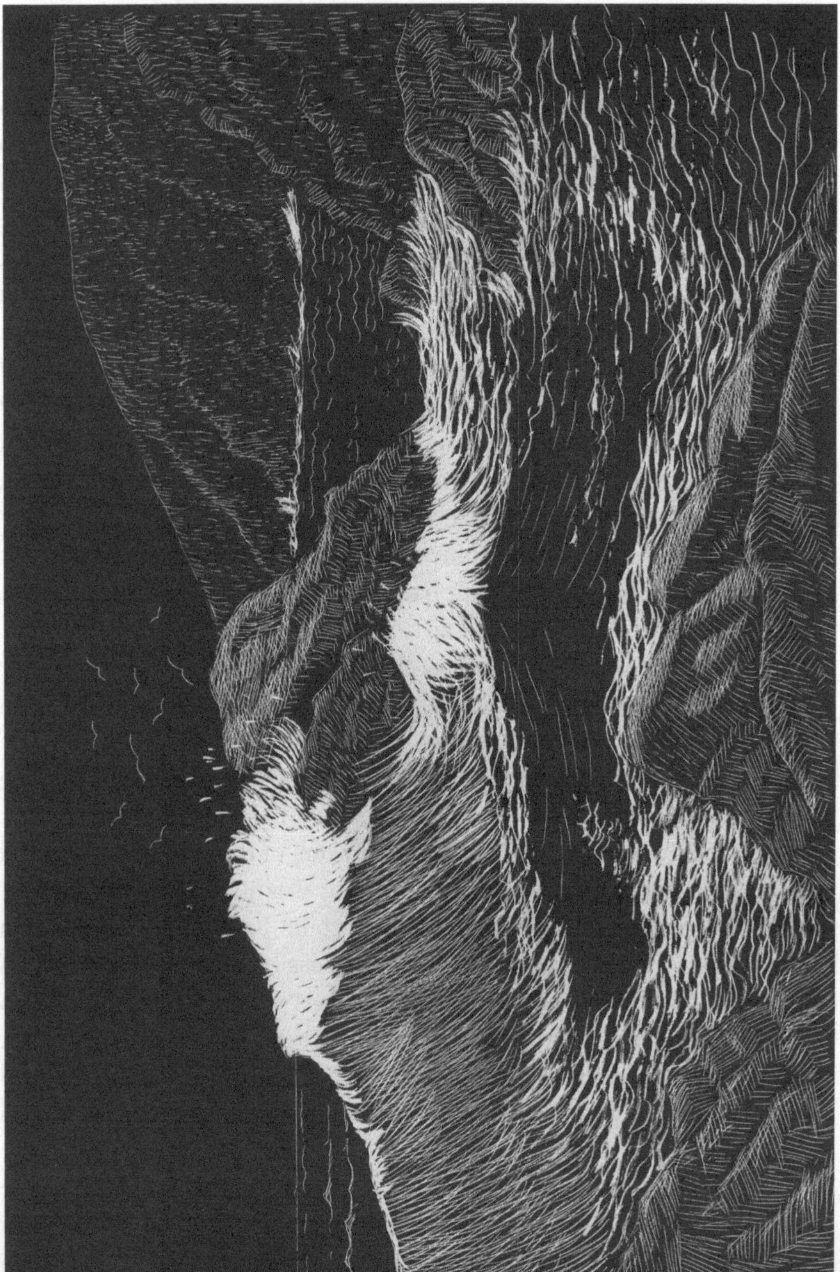

Gideon'. His standard procedure when turning in a confined space was to lift either the front or rear end of the car and carry it to the appropriate place that left the car pointing in the desired direction.

The Model T was in production from 1909 to 1927 and during this time 15,007,003 vehicles were produced, so it was one of the most successful cars ever made. But the Model T could not dominate the car market forever and soon other makes and models, such as the Morris Minor and Austin 7, began to appear.

They all had one thing in common – the gearing system. The epicyclic gearing system used on the Model T had been abandoned. This had used only three gears – slow, fast and reverse – and changing gear was done by pressing or releasing the appropriate pedal. The modern cars had three or four forward gears, which made them more versatile and efficient. However, changing gear required a more complex procedure known as double declutching, which involved using clutch, gear lever and accelerator pedal.

The correct method when changing up a gear was as follows: put out the clutch, close the throttle, take the gear lever to neutral, re-engage the clutch, pause for a second or two – the exact time could only be judged by experience – put out the clutch, put the gear lever into the required gear, re-engage the clutch, open the throttle to take up the drive. The procedure for changing down was even more awkward: put out the clutch, take the gear lever to neutral, re-engage the clutch, use the throttle to speed the engine (to the speed you estimate it would be doing if the car was driving at that road speed in the required gear), put out the clutch and close the throttle, put the gear lever into the required gear, carefully let the clutch back and open the throttle to take up the drive. If all went well the gear lever would go smoothly and silently into gear; if your judgement was a bit faulty the change would be a bit noisy; further out still and, especially if you had used too little speed, the box would emit a horrible grinding noise and the lever would refuse to go into gear.

Most drivers took pride in making their changes as silently as possible. It was not particularly difficult, but did require a good deal of practice to achieve proficiency. Unfortunately, a clumsy change was instantly punished by the loud, harsh sound of gears which hit but do not engage.

It was very loud, so the inexperienced driver's embarrassment was very public. This also meant that all the drivers who had learned on the Model T had to learn the gear-changing system over again. Inevitably this type of gearbox came to be called the crash-box. It is said that one prominent Lerwick driver never did master it and instead used a system of his own, putting the gear lever into the required gear directly, while allowing the clutch to slip by a carefully adjusted amount. I can't help thinking that this must have been more difficult to learn than double declutching, though I have sometimes used a variation of it on the rare occasions when forced to change down into the lowest gear. It is then quite easy to do as by that time the vehicle will be almost at a standstill.

An accessory which was available at the time was the Hold Ford. This attached to the footbrake and allowed it to be locked on like a handbrake. Why it should have been needed in the first place is a bit of a mystery as the Model T already had a handbrake. Whatever the reason it is probably now lost in the mists of time. But Willie was once driving a car which had one of these gadgets fitted. He was heading through West Yell when he came to a gate and had to get out to open it. He set the Hold Ford to keep the car stationary while he went out. Suddenly he heard a sound behind him and looked round to see the car already on the move. He could only watch helplessly as it ran off the road and into a field of corn, where it finally stopped. He walked to it, restarted and drove it back onto the road again and onwards to his destination. One would have expected the owner of the field to be by no means pleased about the incident, but no furious letters or demands from lawyers ever arrived and Willie never heard from him again. However, Willie was never again tempted to depend on Hold Ford.

Cars were subject to many faults and problems which have been largely overcome today and broken half shafts were quite a common occurrence on these early cars. The half shaft is one of the driving rods that connects the two rear wheels to the differential gear; a broken one not only means that the car cannot be driven, but as the footbrake on a Model T operated on the drive shaft it also prevented the footbrake from working. One would have expected it to happen most often when maximum strain was put on them, which would have been when driving up or down a steep hill, but for some reason this was not so. Instead, it happened more often when driving on an almost level stretch of road. Perhaps minor humps and hollows in the road caused the strain to be constantly changing its direction.

An unfortunate incident occurred in the West Yell area when Willie's car suffered a broken half shaft. It happened at a part of the road which was almost level so he managed to get out and put a large stone to one of the wheels to stop the car running away. He was living in West Sandwick at that time and thought he would have to get the car back to his garage there before he could start to repair it. The problem was how to do this with no engine drive and no brakes.

He asked a friend of his, Johnny Leask, who had a hiring business in West Sandwick, to do the towing. Here we come to another minor mystery, again connected with the handbrake. The handbrake operated directly on the rear wheels. There seems no obvious reason why it should not have been used to control the speed of the car being towed, but for some reason this was not done. They were both very experienced Model T drivers so there must have been some good reason why they did not consider this to be a good idea. The book of the Ford does emphasise that the handbrake should be used not to slow or stop the vehicle, but to hold it in place when it is stationary. It does, however, allow it to be used as an emergency brake. Perhaps the drivers thought that it would be better if they kept it for a real emergency.

Whatever the reason, they set off hoping for the best. All went well on the level or slightly uphill, but when they came to a downhill slope Willie's car began to slowly catch up with Johnny's. Johnny would glance over his shoulder and see the rope begin to slacken. The great fear was that the towed car would run over the tow rope which would have left both cars in a very awkward position. Seeing the rope slacken, Johnny would increase his speed, but it was easy to overcorrect by using too much speed which, of course, made Willie's car go faster still. They may have set a new record speed for Model T Fords in Yell, but we don't know for it is extremely unlikely that either car had a speedometer. These were only an optional extra, and at 55 shillings (almost £3) were not cheap. Eventually Willie's garage came into sight and, fortunately, as it was up a slight slope it was easy to come to rest there, to both drivers' great relief. Replacement of the half shaft would not have been easy, especially if it had to be worked on after darkness had fallen.

It was only later that Willie had a disturbing thought. There was not much traffic in Yell at that time but there was one driver who laboured under the delusion that if a head-on collision seemed imminent the thing to do was stop in the middle of the road and blow the horn. All legal requirements, he considered, had then been met. Fortunately, he did not appear on the run to the garage as it would have certainly caused a very awkward situation for all three drivers.

Willie did come close to having a very nasty accident on another occasion. He was driving through Burravoe when he overtook an elderly man pushing a wheelbarrow close to the left-hand side of the road. Just as he was preparing to overtake, the man suddenly turned right to cross the road. Willie managed to avoid him but not the wheelbarrow, the remains of which were thrown off the road in a severely damaged condition. Willie stopped and got out to speak to the man, who excused himself by saying that he was very deaf and had not heard the car's approach. Willie was badly shaken but strongly advised him to always stick to one side of the road and, if he had to cross it, to stop and look both ways first.

For the motorist, financial restraints meant that almost all the cars in Yell at that time were what might well be described as old bangers, and improvisation continued to be a recurrent theme. Before the days of the MOT almost any vehicle which was able to move under its own power was pressed into service.

Many improvisations came under the category of 'It might just happen to work', which inspired the title of this book. One that definitely did was the time Willie's car suffered a puncture in a remote part of the island. He did not have a spare or even a Stepney. Looking around while seeking inspiration he was struck by the amount of long heather growing alongside the road. How about removing the tube, then stuffing as much heather as possible into the tyre? He decided to try it and, strange to say, it did work, at least to the extent of allowing him to drive home, which was all that was required of it.

Once when Willie was driving in the dark in a lonely part of the island he saw a light approaching in the distance. It was rather a strange light, reddish and not very bright, but the most noticeable feature was its motion – it seemed to be swinging left and right in a way that did not suggest any kind of motor vehicle. Willie continued cautiously and eventually his headlights showed up another Model T coming towards him. He stopped and waited until it drew level when he saw it was another pioneer motorist. All his lights had suddenly failed and he had to resort to using a hand-held lantern tied to the radiator cap. It was thus free to swing from side to side, giving the strange effect Willie had noticed. These hand lanterns gave little more light than a candle and without a reflector must have been a poor substitute for the headlamps, but the motorists of those days were well used to that sort of improvisation so he would have taken it in his stride.

It was by no means uncommon for a chassis to have been broken and repaired by bolting on a fence post. Sometimes there had been more than one break repaired in this way, so that the whole frame became a bit fragile and unsteady.

Exhaust pipes were repaired by cutting sheets of tinplate – old National Dried Milk tins salvaged after the war were a popular source of this – which was wrapped round the damaged part of the pipe and held in place by lengths of steel wire, wound round and the ends twisted using pliers. The wire had also probably been recycled from old box wrappings. Small bodywork repairs could be carried out in the same way but these had to be riveted in place, which called for some skill and, worse still, expenditure on the rivets, or whatever was used as a substitute. Incidentally, the milk cans were also used to make model boats which were much enjoyed by the young boys of the district, who sometimes even organised races with them.

Tyres were a constant problem as they were expensive and had a limited life on the extremely rough roads. No-one ever thought of replacing them till they were worn right through to the canvas. Sometimes gaiters, made from pieces of old tyre cut down and fitted inside the existing tyres, were used to extend their life. Brake linings seem to have been a common source of trouble too. Once when Willie was fitting replacements the remains of the old ones came out in 10 pieces.

Kaywick, North-a-Voe, Yell.

One story will illustrate the kind of old bangers then in use. I have given the people involved assumed names. One lady, Jane I will call her, was driving up a slope in North-a-Voe when she had the misfortune to slip off the road. Her attempts to drive back onto the road proved unsuccessful and, on this beautiful summer evening, were so noisy that they attracted the attention of a neighbour – we will call him Frank – who came to see what had happened. He was an experienced driver and offered to take over from Jane and see if he could do better. Jane readily agreed to this so Frank got into the driver's seat and started the engine. He soon discovered two problems: first, the engine was only running on three cylinders; second, the handbrake was not working at all. Here his experience of driving old wrecks came to his aid. Using his right foot on the accelerator, and his left foot – heel on the brake and toe on the clutch – he managed to get the car moving and after a few attempts managed to get it back on the road. He then drove the short distance to the nearest level stretch of road before handing over to Jane, who drove off without any trouble.

A few days later Frank was driving on the road to Mid Yell when he saw Jane in the mirror, still in the same car, pull out and increase speed to overtake him. As she drew level there was a thunderous bang, like an explosion, and her car slowly ground to a halt. Frank stopped, got out and walked back to see what had happened. Jane was still trying to re-start the engine, with noises that might have been caused by a ship going ashore. Frank knew that something serious had happened and persuaded her to stop; the car was obviously not going to start and trying repeatedly would probably do more harm than good. Her husband was working not far away so she decided to walk over and speak to him while Frank continued on his journey. However, as Frank had suspected, the damage to Jane's car's engine proved terminal. Fitting a replacement engine would have cost more than the car was worth. For this old banger it really was the end of the road.

Jane did obtain another car in somewhat similar condition – although it had, in addition, a burst silencer – and continued to drive for years. Another lady who lived not far from Jane had a car which looked to be in quite good condition but if you had to enter it you found otherwise, as the most distinctive feature inside was the smell of petrol; very worrying for any passengers, but no fire ever took place.

Incidentally, when front-wheel drive for cars first became popular some drivers had a curious theory that these would provide less grip than rear-wheel drive and so would be less effective on icy or snow-covered roads. Some went so far as to reverse up steep parts of roads so affected, which must have been very awkward. Some even boasted of their ingenuity and its great success. However, at the same time, many others continued to drive forwards as before and did not seem to have any particular problems.

A number of hiring cars eventually arrived in Yell, and several taxi firms were formed. One of these was operated by Robert Hugh – usually known as Bobby Hugh – Williamson, based in Burravoe. One evening he had taken a group of people to a function in the West Sandwick hall. There were, of course, a number of West Sandwick residents also attending the event. One of them was Hughie, then aged 12.

Bobby Hugh had left his car unattended with the keys still in place, as was the usual practice at that time as there was little crime, and what would be the point of stealing a car if you could not take it off the island? Unfortunately, Hughie, still young enough to be intrigued by anything to do with motor transport, yielded to temptation. Sneaking out from the function he started up the car and set off on a trial run. He drove to the top of a nearby hill, turned and came back to the hall. With great skill, considering his youth and the fact that it was an unfamiliar vehicle, he managed to park it so neatly that Bobby Hugh never suspected that it had been moved. Many years later, long after they had all retired, Willie related this incident to Bobby Hugh who confirmed that this was the first time he ever knew that it had happened.

Willie was often asked to give driving lessons to people, almost all men in those days, who had recently acquired motor cars. One of them was Captain Campbell, a tall, spare Scotsman who had married someone from the Mid Yell area. He was now in his 60s and preparing to learn to drive for the first time. He was a decidedly inept pupil, which Willie found frustrating, but Kari was well pleased as she enjoyed a car ride and always accompanied them.

One summer Sunday morning there was another passenger, a young man who had been badly injured in an accident and was just beginning to walk again using crutches. He got into the back seat alongside Kari. Captain Campbell got into the driver's seat and started the engine. Suddenly the car gave a gigantic bound forward, Kari was thrown backwards, legs in the air, narrowly missing the back of Captain Campbell's head, while the young convalescent roared with laughter.

Some days later the captain came to Willie's house, which was on the side of a steep hill, to arrange another lesson. As Willie and he were walking back down the hill Kari, who had been playing with some old tyres, accidentally dislodged a large truck tyre which set off after them. Kari's shouts of warning went unheard and it was only at the last minute that they realised what was happening and jumped clear. The captain took it very calmly: "Got to be careful with these things," was all he said.

Roads of a Sort

Roads of a sort had existed since the days of the horse and cart but with the coming of powered vehicles they had to be upgraded. In the time of the early motorbikes they were mainly made of gravel, still single track of course, and needed endless attention to be kept usable at all. A group of men were recruited to maintain the roads and carry out minor repairs. There must have been at least three of them in Yell for on one occasion a group of people were discussing the roads and someone wondered who they were. "I know them all," one of the others answered him, "there's Thingamabob and Whatdoyoucall'im and that old devil from the Herra."

In the 1930s an extra road had been built in North-a-Voe at a time when horses were still being used for transport, so an extra roadman was employed especially to drive and look after them. He was Richard Russell, a cousin of Willie's future wife Tamar Mann. He is said to have been the last person ever employed in Shetland in this capacity. The road is still much used, particularly in wintry conditions, to avoid the alternative route through the very steep and awkward 'Kings Road' and the Camb road. Though completed in the 1930s it is still always called the New Road.

The coming of the first cars increased the problems with the surfaces and one of the roadmen was heard to express the view that, "These cars should never have been allowed on the roads."

Dust was a constant problem. In summer, approaching cars were heralded by a huge dust cloud like stampeding cattle in a Western. The dust got everywhere. Under the mudguards it would be caked an inch or more deep, and it formed in great lumps on the cables and pipes underneath the floor and could only be cleaned with great difficulty, especially if there was no hose available, which was usually the case. Older drivers may still remember the trouble they had with potholes: there were usually two rows, one in each of the vehicle tracks. The road at the head of Mid Yell Voe had so many potholes that it came to be known as the 'Lake District'.

But in early motorcycling days the most serious problem seems to have been with ruts. When they froze they became very hazardous to motorcycles. Willie once came upon a young man who had encountered a patch of them and been precipitated into the ditch. After making sure that he had not been injured, Willie helped him back onto the road and asked him what had happened. "Someone told me," the young man said, "that the best way to deal with ruts was to drive over them as fast as possible. That way you would be over them before you had time to fall off. I suppose," he added, "that I was just not going fast enough!"

By the end of the 1950s some improvements began to be made to the notorious Yell roads. The gravel roads with their potholes began to be replaced by tarmacadam, which had previously only been used on two short stretches – one in Mid Yell and one in Burravoe. And the hated gates were replaced by cattle grids. Fortunately, Kari had retired from her business years before.

Some people related horror stories about sheep breaking their legs by getting stuck in the grids, but these seemed to be, to put it mildly, exaggerated. I do not recall any such thing happening in Yell. Also at this time the first policeman was stationed in Yell. The first thing you noticed after this was the number of people who had never passed a driving test. It was quite legal at that time to drive in Yell with only a provisional licence, and without being accompanied by a fully qualified driver. A whole forest of L-plates sprang up overnight, even on the road-roller.

Meanwhile, the same procedures were happening in Unst. Someone decided that it would be a good thing to have a grid fitted on a stretch of road in Uyeasound. If there had been a gate there before it would probably have been replaced with a grid as that seemed to be council policy at that time, but there never had been a gate there. Someone had the bright idea of setting up a gate – it was really only a token gate – in the hope that this too would be replaced. The snag was that drivers of the period hated it and though they had to open it for access they very rarely closed it. No grid ever appeared and eventually one of the drivers became so frustrated that he tore the gate off its hinges and broke it up – easily done as it was so flimsy and poorly constructed – and threw the remains into the nearby loch. So that was the end of the Uyeasound gate and the grid that never was.

Driving for a Living

At one time Willie was employed as chauffeur/handyman by a North-a-Voe shopkeeper, who seems to have had no mechanical knowledge whatsoever and kept asking Willie strange questions about what he regarded as faults. Once he asked about some perfectly normal sound he had noticed. "It is nothing," Willie answered, "just water in the radiator."

"What?" the shopkeeper exclaimed in horror. "Surely not! Water in the radiator of a new car?"

His ignorance seems not to have been confined to motoring. He had at one time been a sailor and it is said that once when the captain gave the order "Port," he replied, "What port? There's no port in sight."

One woman who was a frequent passenger had a habit of asking Willie what might be called 'leading questions' designed to find out how well the shop was doing. Willie usually could not answer them as he knew little about the finances of the shop, but the woman was careful to avoid appearing guilty of idle curiosity and always ended her inquiry with, "Not that I'm caring, you know."

On one occasion Willie's brother-in-law Johnny Mann had arranged to take the shopkeeper to Mid Yell. When Johnny arrived to pick him up the shopkeeper, who seemed to be a bit hazy on medical matters, had changed his mind: "I have started with a cold, and if I go out in a cold wind it might turn to concussion on my chest."

Of course, many elderly people were a little nervous of travelling in these strange machines at all and anything which seemed out of the ordinary was liable to worry them. Willie was always a very careful driver and, in any case, the condition of the roads made any attempt at high speed impossible. However, it was sometimes necessary to turn the steering wheel quite quickly. One day Willie was transporting an elderly lady and had to make a sharp turn at a road junction. As he spun the wheel to take the turn his passenger rebuked him: "Now, now, I don't like your wild steering."

Driving the mails was considered particularly important. One night, when Willie was to do this the following day, his car unfortunately suffered a burned out big-end bearing. He had to work until 2am to fit a replacement. Late nights were common though and on another occasion he worked all night to repair a friend, Bob Mouat's car, though I have forgotten what was wrong with it. Worse still was the time Willie went off the road in icy conditions with the mail aboard, which meant unloading the mail before trying to get the vehicle back on the road again.

Commercial travellers who carried large hampers with samples were frequent customers, and one of them once disputed the mileage he had been charged for. He had measured the distance on a map by using one of the wheeled gadgets which are sold for this purpose. Willie pointed out that because of the small scale of the map it did not show every twist and turn of the road so it would always measure the distance to be shorter than the reality.

On another occasion Willie was driving two travellers, one of whom had not been to Shetland before. At that time the Greenland whaling was still in operation and there was a whaling station at Collafirth. The experienced traveller was telling the newcomer horror stories about the smell they would experience when they came to this station. As they approached it he started to wind down the window then turned to the novice and said, "Now, listen for the smell." It probably was not necessary or desirable to listen too intently!

Another mishap Willie had while driving travellers was the time he had a puncture and had to resort to using the Stepney spare wheel. It clamped on to the side of the existing wheel and was fine in dry weather but the Stepney, unavoidably, was outside the mudguard and on this occasion it was raining so the mud was thrown up over the side of the car. The travellers' hampers were large and protruded over the side of the car and inevitably got rather dirty, which caused Willie some embarrassment and also the work of trying to clean it up.

It has to be said that many of the books describing how to drive the cars of those days encouraged the driver to freewheel as much as possible as it helped to cool the engine. Many years later Willie pointed out to me a place where it was usual to take the car out of gear. It was then possible to freewheel all the way to Burravoe, though at one point you had to allow it to reach quite a high speed to make the distance.

In the days when the small steamer, the *Earl of Zetland*, ran between the islands carrying goods and passengers, none of the piers in Yell had deep enough water for her to come alongside so they anchored some way off and smaller vessels, known as flitboats, carried the cargo and any passengers to the pier. Some piers, such as the one at Cullivoe, were fitted with rail tracks so that a small carriage device could be used to carry the goods up to the top of the pier. It was common practice for vehicles to muster in this area to await their expected cargo.

One problem with the Model T was that if it was left too long in cold weather with the engine stopped, oil was liable to congeal on the surfaces of the clutch causing it to stick. Attempts to start the engine using the starting handle meant that the driver was, in effect, turning the whole transmission right back to the rear wheels. The simplest way to deal with this was to jack up one or both of the rear wheels. It was simple but potentially hazardous. Unless the front wheels were securely jammed and the rear wheels jacked high enough, the car might slip off the jacks and drive forward when the engine started, right over the unfortunate driver. Nevertheless, it became a common practice when waiting for the *Earl of Zetland* to arrive. Presumably all the drivers were scrupulously careful, for there is no record of any serious accident.

Incidentally, although Willie's disability did not usually affect his driving, on some cars he had to use a block under his right heel to be able to operate the accelerator correctly. But Willie became a very experienced driver as he also drove for a time on the Scottish mainland. At one time he was employed as a driver at the Marine Hotel at North Berwick. They seem to have had quite a large range of vehicles. One had the words 'Max. Speed 12 MPH' prominently displayed on the side. Usually this sort of announcement refers to maximum legal speeds, but Willie determined by experiment that in this case they were literally true. On a level road with full throttle in the highest gear it was just about achievable. The only way to reach a higher speed was by freewheeling down a suitable hill, and when one was encountered Willie and many other drivers always made full use of it.

On another occasion Willie was driving in the dark on a section of road which was the subject of a speed limit. He suddenly realised that, very untypically for him, he was driving above the legal speed. At the same time he saw a policeman watching the traffic. Then he remembered that this car had had its old wick rear lamps replaced by electric lights. The rear lamp switch was on the dashboard so he simply switched it off so that the policeman would not be able to read the car number. A bit further on and he was stopped by another policeman who asked him if he had seen any cars driving at excessive speed. Willie replied, quite truthfully, that he had not.

At another time he was employed as chauffeur by Sir James Simpson. The family seem to have been fond of picnics, though these seem to have been not infrequently interrupted by swarms of mosquitoes. On one occasion Sir James's brother caused a minor diplomatic upset by commandeering Willie to take the entire staff on a picnic, leaving Willie in a decidedly awkward position.

How to Drive a Motor Car

As much of this book concerns motoring or motorcycling in the first half of the 20th century, many regulations and the names of parts of equipment may not be readily understood by modern readers. I have tried as far as possible to explain these where they occur in the text, and hope that any which may have been missed will be answered in this chapter.

Anyone learning to drive today can be forgiven for looking at the mass of regulations which cover the subject and wishing they had been born in an earlier age, when motoring was simpler. Suppose, for example, you had lived in the early years of the 20th century. Unless you were particularly well-off your choice of car would have been limited to the Model T Ford, new or second-hand.

You might also have bought a few copies of the available books on the subject, at the price of a few shillings. Usually they started off writing about ordering and taking delivery of your new purchase. Number plates were not essential; the numbers could be simply painted on. One writer, however, advises against this, one reason being, rather surprisingly, that: "When you sell the car you will probably not wish to transfer the number to the buyer."

Insurance was not essential but was strongly recommended – about £8/10 for all risks – and the annual road tax was £6/6. You also had to have a driving licence, but I have not been able to find out the cost of this.

The next step was to learn to drive. Most of the instructions given in these books concern the use of clutch and gears, which were quite different to those on later cars. They were in many ways simpler than later designs. The Ford Model T was designed as a 'people's' car so any unnecessary complications were to be avoided. There were only three gears – slow, fast, and reverse. And changing gear usually involved little more than depressing or releasing the appropriate pedal. However, there were practical problems with this simple system, as you would encounter when you read the main text of the book, so this type of gearbox – the epicyclic – was soon abandoned, with later cars usually using three or four forward gears.

Most books of this period tell us little about steering, but one does advise: "Don't grab the wheel as if it were a lifebuoy, the only thing between you and sudden death. It is quite simple, though it seems very responsible work at first. In fact it soon becomes largely automatic, with our built-in computer doing most of the work."

It was not until May 1935 that a law was passed requiring everyone to pass a driving test before being allowed to drive alone. Learners

The Park, North-a-Voe, Yell.

had to hold a provisional licence, be accompanied by a fully qualified driver, and display L-plates on their cars.

Today's readers may not understand the references to wheel chains, sometimes called Parson's chains. These were used to improve traction in periods of ice and snow. They certainly provided a much better grip, but even the manufacturers would not have claimed that they were, what today would be called, user-friendly.

First you had to jack up the driving wheels. Then you took the first chain and tried to push it up over the upper part of the wheel. Of course the mudguard was in the way, and jacks in those days lifted only the wheel, not the car body, so there was not much room. You might manage this bit wearing gloves, but after that it got more fiddly so you had to use your bare hands.

Next, you had to lay yourself down on your back in the snow and try to creep underneath – not easy to do lying on your back – and get hold of the chain ends. There was a lever on one end of the chain, and some free links on the other. You put the lever through the link which you thought would best match the size of the wheel. Then you pushed down the lever until it clicked into place. Then you could creep out and try to do the same with the other side of the chain.

The important thing was to try to get the chain as tight as possible. The snag was that, after your struggles with bare hands on cold metal, your hands (tiny or otherwise) were frozen and no longer had the strength they needed. You got the chain as tight as you could but, even so, you never got very far before you heard the clink of one of the spare links hitting the mudguard. Then you had to get out and try to tighten them a bit further on, and the performance would have to be repeated again.

Finally, as the last chore, perhaps the last insult, when you no longer needed them you had to take them off as soon as possible as they wore rapidly if used on bare roads.

The Peat Hill

Peat was still commonly used as a fuel and had to be dug out by hand using an implement called a tushker, a job which required a good deal of skill and considerable strength. Most people took some pride in making a neat job of this and it did help with the most unpopular part of the process – raising – when after a few days the oblong chunks of peat were propped up against each other, leaving space for the wind to blow through to complete the drying process.

Some people who were gluttons for punishment also turned them; that is to say after another week or so they rearranged the peats to help the drying process. Not everyone bothered to do this, but one woman was heard to say, "Some people laugh at me for turning the peats, but it really pays you in the end." Most of this work had to be carried out bent double, which made it very painful for anyone with any form of back trouble.

After this the peats usually had to be transported by wheelbarrow to a suitable point as near to the road as possible, to be picked up and transported to the owners' homes by lorries, which had come into common use in Yell. When the great day came a gang of people – men, women and children, it was definitely an equal opportunities employment – were gathered to load the vehicle. This was usually done by throwing the peats into the open back of the lorry. Sometimes a wicker basket, called a kishie, was filled with small peats then emptied into the lorry. However it was done, it was a slow and labour-intensive business.

Willie was often called on to act as driver, and usually was expected to help with the loading as well. This was all very well if a sufficiently large crowd of helpers had been gathered, but more often than not it had not been. It was not unusual for him to arrive at the pick-up point and find only one or two helpers in place. In these circumstances the loading process seemed never-ending.

There were two haulage firms who provided this service: one charged according to the time, which was sensible, but the other charged by the number of loads. If too few loaders had been recruited, the process was hardly worth the driver's time. It was not always a pleasant occupation either. All very well in fine weather, but wet combined with calm was the worst nightmare because as soon as anyone started removing peats from the 'roog' (the heap of peats where the wheelbarrows had been emptied) a swarm of midges would arise to attack the workers. In self-defence they had to keep rubbing their faces, but the wet peat dust clung to their hands and became transferred to their faces and they soon came to resemble a troupe of old fashioned minstrels. In those days, long before most houses had showers fitted, it was a dirty and unpleasant job. It was not surprising that most drivers were very reluctant to become involved with the business.

While the loading process was going ahead it was essential to keep a close watch on the truck wheels. Soft spots on the roads were common and it was not unusual for the wheels to sink into one of these. At the first sign of this happening the truck had to be moved. Once it had become bogged in it was no easy matter to extricate it. Even when the peats had been driven to their destination the driver's troubles were sometimes not over. A place where the stack was to be built would have been decided and it was not always readily accessible without crossing areas of dubious firmness. It was all too easy to come to disaster on the threshold of success and much depended on the skill of the driver. All things considered, it is not surprising that peat truck transport was one job that most drivers regarded with horror.

One man who lived in a house alongside the main road devised another method of getting his peats home, which today would be praised as environmentally-friendly. No mechanical power was needed at all. His peat banks were close to the top of a hill and, after taking them by wheelbarrow to a point alongside the main road, he built them into a pile. Then he waited for winter and a suitable fall of snow, which was very common in those days. He had made a long sledge with a looped rope for pulling, and was able to load the peats onto it. The way to his house was downhill most of the way and he was able to pull it home without too much difficulty. A minor problem he experienced was that the pile of peats in the hill sometimes suffered damage when some of the upper part slipped off and ran down the side of it. There were a great many motorcycles around at the time and when this happened Robert, the man who owned the peats, always blamed young motorcyclists for leaning their bikes along the pile. This was not entirely fair. It turned out that at least some of the damage was caused by a decidedly elderly vandal. Robert's uncle, Robbie Smith, a retired sea captain, later confessed that he was responsible for at least some of the incidents. He would visit Robert and remark that he'd seen that the peats had fallen again, whereupon Robert would again blame the young motorcyclists.

Willie's nephew, Bobby Smith, had taken up lorry driving and one day was delivering peats to the local school teacher. One of the few perks of peat working was that the workers were usually at some time given a good meal. As they sat down, the teacher asked Bobby how many loads were left to take home. As Bobby was trying to work out an estimate he failed to notice that the teacher, a religious lady, had started to say grace, "For what we are about to receive ..." she began, then Bobby suddenly answered her, "About two lorry loads."

The use of lorries for transport eventually fell out of favour for peat work and using a tractor and trailer became the preferred method. It was more convenient as they were often able to climb up the hill where the peats had been cut and dried, avoiding the tiresome and labour intensive business of moving them to the road by wheelbarrow. Another advantage with the tractor and trailer system was that it was usually easier to deposit the load quite close to where it would be required, and the smaller loads made it easier for the people who were to build the stack to handle them.

The state of the hill was always a matter of some concern. If there had been any rain at all between the time when the peats were cut and the time when they would be taken home, which in reality there almost always was, one rather pessimistic man would always say, "Ah, there will be no peats out of the hill this year." Nevertheless, he always managed to get his peats home.

The hill could become soggy and prone to act as a trap if there had been a lot of rain. The tractor, or more often trailer, would sink in and become firmly stuck. If another tractor was available it was sometimes possible to pull the whole combination back onto a firmer part of the hill, but more often, it had to be freed by shovels and manpower. Much depended on the skill of the driver and a good driver could successfully drive over places which looked impassable. While one's instinct was to take these places slowly and carefully, this gave more time for the weight to press on the soft ground, and could have disastrous results, so it was always advisable to cross doubtful places as quickly as possible.

One time when Willie's peats were being taken home this way, the driver seemed to be crossing a soft patch so slowly that one could actually see the surface of the moor bending. It seemed it could only be a matter of time before the wheels broke through it, but the driver suddenly injured his back and thought he could no longer continue. He arranged for a substitute driver to take over, and in a classic case of an ill wind blowing in no one's favour, the new driver shot across the suspect area like a grand prix driver and had no more trouble. So once again the peats were brought safely home.

After the load had been tipped out at the desired spot the work was still not finished. The next job was to build the peats into a stack. The design of the stack was usually fairly standard but there was a belief that only certain people – well-known in each village – were capable of doing it successfully, though they were expected to use a number of less-skilled assistants. It was believed that if an unqualified person tried to build the stack it would either 'water-drink' – which meant the roof section would leak and cause water to pour into the main body of the stack, damaging or destroying the peats stored within – or 'run', which meant that one or more sections would detach from the main structure and fall in a spread-out heap on the ground. This happened regularly to 'sledge-man' Robert, but in this case it happened spontaneously without any human intervention and without anyone to blame but the incompetent stack-builder.

Eventually some brave souls decided to try their hand at stack-building and found that it was a skill that was not at all difficult to acquire, requiring little more than common sense, a steady hand and care. I never heard of any disasters resulting.

There was not really any reason to make the stack a work of art but most people tried not to make it a blot on the landscape. One day Davy Brown and his brothers were hard at work building their newly delivered peats when some busybody, of the type who seem to think it's their duty to annoy their neighbours by pointing out real or imagined mistakes, arrived and began to criticise their efforts. Eventually Davy had had enough. "It doesn't matter," he said, "we're going to burn this anyway."

Although some people claimed to enjoy it, and even turned it into a picnic outing, with thermos flasks of tea, bottles of lemonade, biscuits and other refreshments, working peats was always a hard and time-consuming business. Eventually, with a modest improvement in living standards, peat fires began to be replaced by oil-fired central heating and fell into decline. In time there was only one man actively engaged in the transport with tractor and trailer, and it became increasingly difficult to find anyone willing to take on the other work involved, from cutting the peat through raising, turning, wheelbarrow delivery to suitable site, filling the lorry or trailer and building the stack.

There were, for some years, businesses that employed people, mainly as seasonal workers, to work peat commercially, using mechanically-cut peat and selling it by the bag. There were also a few people who, perhaps for nostalgic reasons, continued to work a single peat bank to provide fuel for a display fire in their sitting rooms, but notwithstanding the relentlessly increasing cost of all forms of fuel, and not helped by the latest panic about climate change and the using of fossil fuels, the days of using peat seriously as the main fuel for heating houses are probably over.

Working in Lerwick

The coming of war in 1939 brought many changes. Willie's disability made him ineligible for military service. Many years before he had tried to join the RAF but had been turned down for that reason. He was, however, offered a job by MacLeod & MacLean in Lerwick, mainly employed in radio repairs. Of course, in Lerwick most of the radios were mains powered and he was more familiar with battery sets, but the basic principles were just the same and he was soon able to adapt. Sometimes he got involved in solving ordinary electrical problems too, often caused by people who had attempted electrical work without enough knowledge. One such time was when he was called to the house of a man who had fitted a new light in one of the rooms but found it continually blew the fuse. Willie soon found that the switch had been connected across the lamp, instead of in series with it. With the switch turned off the light burned continuously, when switched on it blew the fuse.

The difficulty in obtaining spare parts for radio repairs gave Willie every opportunity to employ his gift for improvisation. He became particularly skilled in rewinding by hand the many radio components, such as speaker transformers, which depend on long windings of very thin wire. These transformers were unobtainable during the war and needed great skill to repair. Many years after the end of the war this skill was pressed into service again when he was called on to rewind the coil of a solenoid from a juke-box, which had proved unobtainable.

Willie sometimes had to help out in the shop and, given the grim times, it was perhaps not surprising when one lady, intending to ask for one of the officially approved black-out torches, accidentally asked Willie if they had any black-outlook torches.

Lerwick was a busy town in wartime with every branch of the services represented. It was not at all unusual for Willie to be called on to carry out repairs on a wide variety of equipment, much of it unfamiliar. One job was on a naval vessel which was under orders to sail at 5am. Willie had completed his repair in good time when the captain accidently knocked part of it off the wall, sending the repairs back to square one. However, Willie managed to redo the repairs successfully and the ship did sail at 5am as directed.

A common sight was the Bren gun carrier, with its thunderous metallic clanking and clanging audible for hundreds of yards. Like all tracked vehicles it proceeded not in a straight line but in a sort of zig-zag path so that when it hove in sight it appeared to weave erratically from side to side. This, together with its quite high speed and tremendous clanking and clanging noise, gave the impression of a wild, uncontrollable monster which the driver was only just managing to hold in check. This impression was perhaps not too far wide of the mark, for there were many accidents and it was by no means unusual to see one lying on its side in a ditch.

Public baths were situated in the Victoria Restaurant at the Market Cross and always seemed to do good business, particularly with servicemen who were often to be seen entering or leaving with their towels over their arms. Presumably washing facilities at the camps were less than perfect. The wall close by seemed to present an irresistible temptation for 'artists' who drew pictures of that enigmatic war-time character Chad. There always seemed to be at least one picture of this mysterious figure making his usual cryptic comments on the situation. Below Fort Charlotte there was a line of colourful posters advertising upcoming films in the local cinema, the North Star.

If questioned as to what they wanted to do when they grew up, most small boys in Lerwick at that time would have chosen to be Spitfire pilots. A popular second choice, however, might well have been a despatch rider – dashing figures in crash-helmet, goggles and full leathers – who tore almost incessantly around the town on noisy motorcycles, at speeds far higher than any other vehicles at that time. If I remember correctly it was Ernie Entwistle, a character in the popular comic *Knockout*, who, on describing someone moving at high speed, came up with a phrase we could all appreciate: "He was going like a despatch rider late for his tea."

Children are very adaptable and few thought that the war posed any threat to their personal safety. If anything was to happen to them it would be like the hero of a book being killed off in the first page. Only rarely was confidence in this simple philosophy rudely shattered. Perhaps the worst occasion was the time the mines came ashore at the Sletts. A winter gale was blowing and the story current at the time was that part of the harbour boom defence had broken loose. Throughout the night all of Lerwick was rocked by a series of terrifying explosions which caused widespread damage to nearby houses. Children from the Sound district had, of course, to pass this area on their way to school and ever after during southeast gales the sea was anxiously scanned for sinister objects.

Placed at strategic points around the town were the so-called road-blocks – wooden structures which effectively closed off half the road. This forced all traffic to pass through in single file under the watchful eyes of armed guards, presumably to prevent suspicious vehicles sneaking in under cover of heavy traffic. The roads were said to be mined at these points and, for children, this belief lent some excitement to passing them. They tiptoed carefully over them then, having got a few yards past, heaved a sigh of relief: "Made it again."

MacLeod & MacLean also had a garage which carried out various kinds of motor repairs, so Willie often was witness to incidents in which he was not personally involved. One of these related to an apprentice who was sent to deliver a motor lawn mower which had just been repaired. Unfortunately no-one had explained to the apprentice that not all the engine controls were situated conveniently close to the hand grips. Some important controls, including a few in the clutch and throttle, were placed some way down on one of the handles. The apprentice had started off at a good speed but he discovered, with the machine already in motion, that he could not reach far enough down to operate the controls so he could not slow the mower, which seemed to be gathering speed all the time. He soon saw that in a race with the mower he was going to finish a poor second. Furthermore, he would tire while the mower would not. It seemed to him that he had run the entire road system of Lerwick and was exhausted when he remembered the short but extremely steep stretch of road known as Cockatoo Brae. With his last reserves of strength he was able to turn the mower in its direction and hold on until he reached the bottom of the brae. It worked. The mower had met its match and ground to a halt, leaving the exhausted apprentice to slowly recover his breath, before driving on to his destination, keeping very carefully at a sedate pace.

Just after the end of the war Willie hired a self-drive car and took his family on a trip down to Sumburgh. This had been a civilian airfield beforehand but was used by the military during the war and was subject to many restrictions. All the restrictions would have been removed by now, or so Willie thought. As they neared their destination they came upon a prominent 'Stop!' notice. He stopped. There was only one person in sight, a woman peacefully taking her dog for a walk. Willie asked her if she knew what the notice meant. She hastened to reassure him, saying that it was an old notice and no longer applied. "It just doesn't appeal to you at all," she finished.

Boat Lands at Kaywick

By 1941 the 'Shetland Bus' operation, which brought many refugees and sometimes returning secret agents from Norway into the UK, was under way. In February or early March a boatload of Norwegian men landed at Kaywick in Yell. It seems impossible to find any written record of this as, being wartime, everything was kept as secret as possible and by now not many people recall the event. After some days a truck arrived and took

Willie Williamson (Snr) and Clara.

Billy's uncle and aunt, Andrew and Ester Williamson.

Willie (Jnr) and Tamar (née Mann) Williamson.

Captain Henry Williamson.

Photo courtesy of Basil Moar

Group at peat stack.

Seafield, North-a-Voe, Yell.

The Williamson Family aunts and uncles. Back: Henry, Georgie, John, Hughie and Willie (missing is Andrew in Australia). Front: Clara and Andrina (missing is Christina in Edinburgh). *Photo courtesy of Irene Moar*

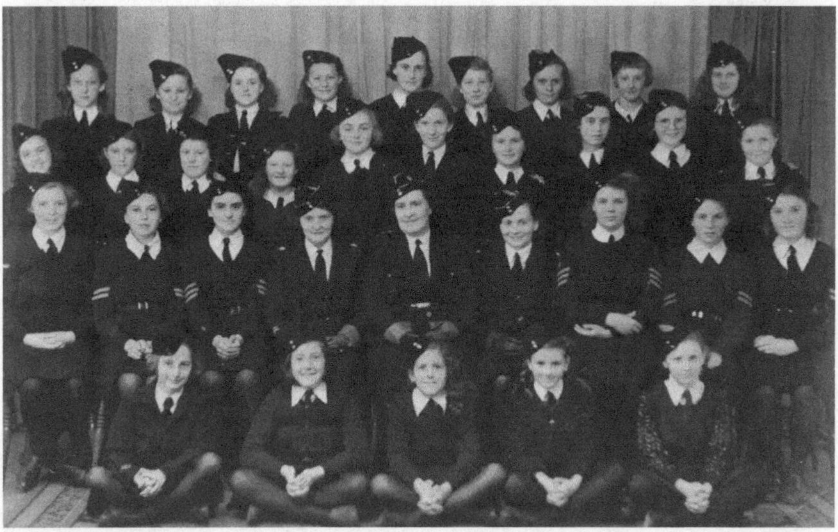

Kari Williamson, front second from right.

Willie Williamson dressed as a chauffeur.

Willie Williamson's Model T Ford, with Tamar Williamson and Joey Stewart.

Kari Williamson (left) and Irene Woodman outside Bellevue, Knab Road, Lerwick.

most of the crew away, probably for interrogation, while the boat itself was taken to Lerwick.

Willie Snr, who lived in West Sandwick, was a recognised pilot and was recruited to pilot the Norwegian boat to Lerwick. 'Aald Daa', as he was called by his grandchildren, was an old haaf-man (that is to say he had taken part in commercial fishing using open boats and sails), so he was entirely familiar with the seas around Shetland, but he knew nothing of the town of Lerwick. However, his son Henry, at that time a merchant navy captain, was home and decided to go on the trip to Lerwick too, in order to escort his father to the house of relatives who lived in Hill Lane where he was to stay until he could get back home to Yell.

At that time there was scarcely a house in Shetland that did not possess what was known as an American clock. They were large mantelpiece clocks powered by weights and had various types of decoration. The one in the Williamson family home had an eagle carved on the top. There was a space behind the bird where any extra money was kept in case of emergencies and Clara, the youngest of the family, then aged 18, could remember her grandfather's fee being put safely away there until required. According to family memory it was 10/- (10 shillings), hardly a generous payment, but it must be remembered that in those days it was worth much more in purchasing power than the modern equivalent of 50 pence.

Fire down below

Sometimes Willie was asked to look at one of the small motor-boats which were in common use in the islands. One of these was owned by two brothers, who told him that, aware of the problems dampness could cause magnetos which were an essential component of engines of that time, they always removed the magneto and took it ashore with them when they left the boat. Unfortunately they did not understand the importance of timing the magneto, so that it produced its spark at the right time. On this engine the magneto was driven by a gearwheel. The timing could be adjusted by turning the gearwheel on its shaft. Amazingly, it had worked for years without trouble. It seems that during all the magneto's removal and refitting the gearwheel had never actually been turned.

Willie soon had it fixed and instructed the brothers how to preserve the engine timing in future.

More serious was the trouble encountered by a man called John who was testing his boat's engine while lying at anchor. He was down in the engine room with the engine running when he noticed that the flywheel seemed to have come loose on its shaft. On a wooden-hulled boat this could have been very serious, so he decided to stop the engine. For some strange reason he did not do this in any conventional method, instead he took hold of the plug leads and pulled them off. All might still have been well if he had held on to them, but HT insulation in those days was sometimes very poor so it is likely that he suffered a shock, and dropped them. They fell on to some straw matting which was soaked in petrol and burst into flames. John wasted no time in scrambling up the ladder and into the wheelhouse. As he came in he remarked casually to Willie, "There's a bit of a fire down there."

Willie looked down into what he regarded as a raging inferno. By great good luck he found a fire extinguisher in the wheelhouse. He soon had the fire under control, and was able to save the boat and its crew from disaster, but it was a very nasty moment.

The Home Guard

Willie Jnr had joined the Home Guard some years before he moved to Lerwick, and he discovered that he was a fine marksman. One night he and another man (I am not sure of his name but we can call him John) were on guard at Lerwick Harbour. As they gazed at the dark water John said, "What would you do if we saw the German Fleet steaming in the harbour mouth?"

"Well," Willie replied, "I suppose we would be expected to stick to our post and try to defend the town."

"You can stay if you want," said John, "but I'll be out that door like lightning. One shell and this building will disappear. What can two men with rifles possibly do to stop them?"

Fortunately it never happened so they did not have to make any decision.

For some mysterious reason Yell, the second largest island in the Shetland Isles, and situated between the strategically important bases of Unst and Sullom Voe, never had a military base of any sort. Any protection for Yell had to be provided by the Home Guard. If an emergency occurred Willie, at that time still living in Yell, was always one of the first to be contacted as he drove a truck and could drive around and collect the other members. One particularly scary occasion was the night that one of them, Jimmy Willie Spence, arrived at Utterabister where Willie was staying. After rousing him he went to the other house of Utterabister where he thought Richard Russell was staying, hammered on the window and shouted, "Ritchie! We've been called out. The buggers have left Norway."

As it happened, Jimmy had woken not Richard Russell (a cousin of Willie's wife Tamar and a senior Home Guard member who had served in the navy in the First World War) as he had intended, but the grandmother of the family, Jemima Mann. She was elderly and had the sight of only one eye. She had had a hard life, being widowed and having lost two very young children, but she was pretty tough so she was probably not too disturbed. Nevertheless, although we may laugh at it today, it must have been very frightening at that time.

The trouble with these rumours was that they were so plausible. Looking at the map it seems very likely that if the Nazis really did decide to invade Britain via Shetland, as at one time was considered a distinct possibility, their invasion point would almost certainly be the large, undefended island of Yell.

The Home Guard also sometimes had to deal with incidents which, though not perhaps so startling as the arrival of enemy troops and the start of the invasion, were not false alarms. One such was the time a Seafire fighter had to make a forced landing in Basta, close to the voe. His improvised landing strip turned out to be slightly too short and after running some distance along it he hit a rough patch and the aircraft tipped over on its nose and fell on its back.

The pilot was uninjured and there was no fire, so he managed to scramble out to be met by two men who had witnessed the accident. The elder man was worried in case someone had been lost. "Are you sure there is no-one else pinned down underneath her?" he asked.

"If there is, I know nothing about them," joked the pilot, who then asked if there was any military base nearby. The elder of the two told him that there was not, but he also said that the younger man, David Nisbet, was a member of the Home Guard.

The pilot then took charge and told David to go home for his kit then come back and mount an armed guard until other arrangements could be made. David did so. He did not expect any trouble, but a policeman who should have known better insisted on climbing into the plane. David, who was afraid that he might accidentally fire the guns, absolutely forbade this and finally had to threaten him with his bayonet. After that he had no trouble and soon other members of the Home Guard came to relieve him and a regular rota was set up until the wreck was removed by sea some time later.

A far more serious and much grimmer incident, also involving an aircraft, had occurred when a Catalina flying boat crashed in a remote part of south Yell in 1942. The Catalina was a large aircraft. Built by the Consolidated Aircraft Corporation of San Diego, California, it was 62ft long with a wingspan of 104ft. Powered by two 1,200hp engines it had a maximum speed of 200 mph and a range of 4,000 miles. Over 3,000 were built, more than any other flying boat before or since, and they became one of the mainstays of Coastal Command.

This one turned out to be Catalina Z2148 of 240 Squadron Coastal Command. It had taken off in the early hours of the morning, from Loch Erne in Northern Ireland, on a mission to locate the new German battleship *Tirpitz* which at that time was suspected of lurking in the Norwegian fjords. After refuelling at Invergordon the Catalina proceeded north into the search area. Because of the length of the mission it carried an extended crew of 10: the pilot, Flight Lieut Harry Goolden; co-pilot Flight Lieut Alexander Helme; navigator, Pilot Officer L.G. Schell; Sgt E. Henowy; Sgt L.A. Rowe; Sgt Lex Irvine; Sgt A. Pitcher; Sgt R. Breakspear; a/c mechanic Jock Richmond; and Flight Sgt Dan Lockyer.

Bad weather and engine trouble forced the mission to be abandoned and the pilot decided to head for the nearest RAF base, which happened to be Sullom Voe. They reported by radio to Sullom Voe and requested a flare path be lit to help with their landing, but for some reason this was

Old church and manse West Sandwick, Yell.

never done. As they had by then lost too much height, the pilot took the aircraft out over the sea to circle and gain more height before attempting to land. In the darkness, and with heavy snow showers, they somehow became disoriented and came in slightly too far north, which brought them over the island of Yell. They had almost made it across the island when a sudden gust of wind brought them down on the hill.

The aircraft did not fly into the hill but slid along it for some distance, with parts breaking off. Then it fell over on its side and burst into flames. Flight Sgt Lockyer – one of the radio operators – managed to escape from the wreck then courageously went back in and dragged out the injured co-pilot, Flight Lieut Helme, which was no mean feat as he was a big, heavy man.

Though Lockyer had injured his ankle and lost his boots in the crash he tried to go back into the aircraft a second time to look for more survivors. But he was driven back by the flames so decided to set off walking downhill to try to reach some habitation where he could raise the alarm. After a nightmare journey, in the course of which he fell into a burn and was soaked to the skin, he came to the house of Arisdale. By that time he was unable to stand and had to crawl the last few yards. He managed to knock on the door, which was answered by Brucie Henderson (who was later to become very well-known and was interviewed on radio as a teller of folklore stories) who helped Lockyer into the house. He was able to relate his story to Brucie who, with his wife Katy, made him comfortable for the night, before Brucie set off next morning to raise the alarm.

As it turned out the crash had been witnessed independently by a group of Home Guards stationed at the Burravoe Hall, so the rescue mission would have been carried out even if Lockyer had not managed to complete his epic walk. Their first task was to carry the injured men down to the inhabited part of the nearest village of Burravoe. As well as Helme they discovered another survivor: a/c mechanic Jock Richmond had been in the tail section of the aircraft which broke off when it struck the ground so was not touched by the flames. He was not able to walk as he had suffered a broken leg, but the Home Guard soon carried him to safety. The next day they had the gruesome task of carrying down the bodies of the seven fatalities. It was originally intended to take these to the Shetland Mainland for burial in one of the war graves there, but bad weather again intervened, with stormy sea conditions making it impossible for any boats to cross Yell Sound. In the end they were buried in the church yard at Hamnavoe, where they still remain. At that time the grave was marked by a simple wooden cross, to which an engraved brass plate was later added. For his actions that night Flight Sgt Lockyer was awarded the British Empire Medal, Military Division.

The Home Guard came in for a good deal of criticism and even ridicule at that time, and years later almost everyone enjoyed *Dad's Army* on TV. Probably many of the exploits involving Captain Mainwaring and his colleagues were not all that much exaggerated, but we should not forget that they sometimes also did really useful and often extremely unpleasant work

Unlike the Seafire crash there was never any question of salvaging the Catalina. It came down in a remote and inaccessible area where miles of very rough country separated it from the nearest road. In any case, the fire had caused so much damage that there was almost nothing left worth salvaging. It was left on the hillside where it fell and remained undisturbed, except for occasional visits from relatives of the men who lost their lives, or some who were interested in Shetland's aviation history.

The wreckage lies in a very bare and featureless area and, for anyone not familiar with this part of the hills, could be very difficult to find. As the 50th anniversary of the crash approached some interested people began to discuss the possibility of erecting a memorial on the site. A public meeting was held in the Old Haa and the Catalina Memorial Committee was formed. It was decided to erect a nine-foot stainless-steel cross with a descriptive plaque to serve both as a marker and as a memorial to the men who died. Hamish Polson, one of the committee, designed it and it was built by a local engineering firm. The logistical problem of transporting it safely to the site was solved when a small helicopter, used by Shetland Islands Council for anti-pollution work, was offered for this purpose.

A dedication ceremony conducted by the Rev. Magnus Williamson was held on 25th August 1991. Dan Lockyer had travelled north for the service and, as the climax, laid a wreath at the foot of the cross in memory of his fallen comrades. About 160 people attended the service. Many of them had walked from Arisdale following, in reverse, the route used by Lockyer almost 50 years before, but this time in the much more pleasant conditions of a fine summer day. However, the helicopter was again used to carry to the site those who were not fit enough to attempt the walk. They included Mrs Mary Goolden, widow of the pilot. When she died several years later her ashes were interred in her husband's grave in accordance with her wishes.

Later, a line of fence posts with white painted tops were installed to help as a guide for walkers to find the memorial. A propeller blade from the Catalina and a memorial plaque were also erected outside the Old Haa at Burravoe, which allowed elderly or infirm visitors to read the main facts of the story without having to attempt the challenging walk to the site of the crash.

Radio Times

All the boys in the Williamson family appear to have been what you might call mechanically-minded. Apart from motorcycles, and later cars, they were involved with radios, gramophones, cameras and other symbols of scientific progress. Their first radio used earphones, but the boys soon discovered that after dark (when distant radio signals usually come in more strongly) they could lay the phones in the gramophone horn and use it as a loudspeaker. Donny and Willie both became very interested in the technical side of radio and later worked professionally in this area.

Being a musical family they were particularly interested in the music programmes and, as well as the BBC stations, often listened to the Irish station then called Athlone, and later Radio Eiran, and became very fond of Irish dance music. Much later the younger members of the family came to prefer Radio Luxembourg or AFN American Forces Network. They collected and often played many 78rpm records, both musical and comical. Popular favourites were Harry Lauder, Harry Gordon and the Irish comedian Michael Casey.

Domestic radio played a very important role during the war. Everyone listened to the war news. It was certainly not an expensive hobby, though it was said that one man used to sit by the radio with one hand on the on/off switch and holding his watch in the other. He was then able to see the exact time to switch on the *One o'Clock News*, which was the only programme he ever listened to.

Many people were also keen listeners to the many morale-boosting and light entertainment programmes. Most popular were the comedy programmes, most famously *ITMA*, but there were many others such as *Much-Binding-In-The-Marsh*, *Band Waggon*, *Stand Easy*, *Navy Mixture* and *Children's Hour*, often listened to by adults as well, particularly the *Toytown* stories with Larry the Lamb, Dennis the Dachshund, Ernest the Policeman, the Mayor and Mr Growser. Rather surprising, perhaps, to have a German dog in a starring role. Dennis was not really a villain but he was certainly mischievous and often involved Larry in his dubious schemes. "Come, Larry, my friend, an idea I have, most excellent," was a typical remark, before going on to describe some hare-brained scheme.

Music was provided by *Music While You Work* with Vera Lynn, Anne Shelton, Petula Clark, Glen Miller etc, all providing relief from the grim reality of the war. Rather strangely, there was at least one programme which deliberately set out to frighten the listener. This was *Appointment with Fear*. The fear was not about the war – such a programme would have been considered defeatist, unpatriotic, and would probably have been illegal – but a more primitive one, often supernatural. The programme consisted of a series of scary tales, always introduced and sometimes narrated by the 'Man in Black'. He was played by the inimitable Valentine Dyall, whose voice was so sinister that listening to him was often more scary than the actual stories.

There were many other dramas including *Dick Barton*, *Father Brown*, *Journey into Space*, *Paul Temple*, *P.C. 49*, *Riders of the Range*, *Inspector Duncan* and, included in *Children's Hour* were *Norman and Henry Bones, the Boy Detectives*. They were rather improbably played by Charles Hawtrey as the elder brother Norman, and Patricia Hayes as the younger Henry. There were more crime stories with *The Armchair Detective* and *Inspector Hornleigh Investigates*. For the more intellectually minded there was *The Brains Trust*, the critics' *Any Questions?* and even *Masterspy*.

It was important that people heard the news direct from the radio and did not rely on second-hand information from friends and neighbours. This was impressed on Willie one day when an elderly lady told him, quite seriously, that there had been fierce fighting among the crocuses. It should of course have been the Caucuses. Willie was reminded of a similar situation during the previous war when someone described a day of furious arguments in parliament: "Lloyd George and the prime minister," they said, "have been face to face!" The mistake here was that at that time Lloyd George *was* the prime minister.

During the war the radio had become an indispensable piece of equipment in almost every home in Britain and this continued into the post-war era, the emphasis then being on entertainment rather than news. The only radio available to the general public during the war was the 'civilian' receiver – a very basic model made by a variety of manufacturers and in limited supply – so most of the sets then in use were older models, dating from the 1930s.

There were a bewildering number of manufacturers, almost all of them British: Aerodyne; Beethoven; G.E.C. Cossor; Burndept; Invicta; Pye; Ultra; Bush Murphy; Ferranti; McMichael; K.B. Mullard; Alba; Philco; R.G.D. Pilot; Ekco; Ferguson Berec; Perdio; Roberts; Grundig; as well as more familiar names, such as Marconi, Philips or Ever-Ready. By modern standards they were large. cumbersome beasts with handsome, often heavily veneered, wood cabinets. In radio, as in most other developments, fashion played a part and at one time huge radiograms which combined the radio and gramophone into one unit were popular and were often used as status symbols. But eventually, perhaps because of the amount of space they took up, they went out of favour.

Of course, the radio was not self-contained as it needed external aerial and earth connections. The aerial was a long, stranded copper wire connected to the aerial pole at one end and usually to the chimney stack at the other, via ceramic insulators. Originally they were limited, legally, to 100ft. The down-lead was taken into the house through a lead-in tube: a brass rod passed through an ebonite tube and led through the window frame. Special earth rods were available but, more usually, the earth consisted of any substantial piece of metal buried outside the same window. The wire to it passed through the window frame.

Inside the house both aerial and earth leads were connected to a so-called lightning switch. This resembled a miniature version of the type used in *Frankenstein*. Switched one way it connected the aerial to the radio, switched the other way it connected the aerial to the earth, for use during thunderstorms. Many people were a bit worried about lightning strikes; one man claimed to have seen the lightning coming towards his window before it turned aside when only a foot or two away.

If the receiver was not very sensitive, or you were trying to receive a weak station, you had to rely on a delicate adjustment of the reaction control. Advancing this caused a dramatic increase in sensitivity, but if advanced too far it caused the set to oscillate, producing a loud howling noise which was most unpleasant. It was also illegal as it could, in theory, cause interference in neighbouring receivers, though was only likely to do so if the offending set was of really antiquated design.

All stations were MW or LW, the dials were calibrated in wavelengths, not frequency, and station names were given. A popular additional feature was the so-called 'trawler band' which allowed listeners to hear conversations between the local fishing boats. Willie modified many radios to enable them to receive it. It was quite easy if there was a short wave band already fitted which the owners were prepared to sacrifice; much more difficult if there wasn't.

An obvious problem in rural areas was the lack of a mains power supply. Most of these radios needed three batteries – HT, GB, and a wet accumulator. The HT battery was quite large and provided 120V with tappings for lower voltages. The GB battery was a smaller version of the same and provided 9V, again with several tappings. These batteries were connected to the radio by what were called wander plugs. These were perhaps well named as there was no attempt to make their connection foolproof. They were rarely labelled, though there was a rough colour code: red for positive, black for negative, with various non-standard colours for intermediate connections. There were sometimes as many as seven, so it was quite easy to make a mistake, with disastrous results even, if you were really unlucky, damaging expensive valves. Incidentally, during the war it was not unknown for these colourful plugs to be pressed into service by removing the metal parts and stringing the plastic parts together to make a cheap but colourful necklace.

After the war most radios were of the superhet design. These were not a new idea – they had been invented as long ago as 1919 – but, before the war, they had been expensive luxury items. Now, with more modern manufacturing methods, often devised during the war, they were no more expensive than the older TRF type, gave much better performance and dispensed altogether with the fiddly reaction control.

The accumulator must have been one of the most user-unfriendly devices ever produced. It was a single rechargeable lead-acid cell of the type still used for car batteries. It was housed in a thick glass jar – the size varied according to the accumulator capacity – and connected to the radio via two screw terminals fitted on the top of the device, which were screwed down on spade terminals connected to the radio supply flex. All these terminals were subject to corrosion, even if they were coated with petroleum jelly as was recommended.

Unlike the HT battery, which with normal use could last months and only gradually lost sensitivity before it stopped working, the accumulator died rather abruptly when it needed recharging, losing power and stopping within seconds. If this happened during a tense moment in a boxing match or a Paul Temple mystery drama it could cause agitation until it was removed and the replacement fitted. Often pliers were needed to unscrew the terminals, and then they had to be cleaned, which all took time during which other members of the family sometimes criticised the unfortunate operator for not being better prepared.

In an emergency a twin-cell battery, consisting of two slightly larger-than-normal dry cells, permanently connected in series and used for bicycle headlamps, could be used. These provided 3V, while the accumulator's output was only 2V, so in theory the radio's valves were overrun. However, the internal resistance of a dry battery is higher than that of an accumulator, so it is unlikely the actual voltage was really any higher. The capacity was also much lower so it could only be used for a short time.

One seaman purchased an American radio when he was away. It was rated as using a 110 ac/dc supply so the sailor thought he could power it using a 120V HT battery. The snag was that the radio used far more power when used in this way than with the battery normally supplied. So although it worked, it could only be used for a few hours before the battery became completely discharged.

The accumulator was not sealed and contained sulphuric acid so was not really the sort of thing you would like to have in your home. The acid seemed to creep and was always present to some extent on the top surface. Being diluted it could not cause serious burns to a human being, but it was absolutely fatal to any form of cloth, except perhaps some modern synthetic fibre-based types. Many pairs of lace curtains fell victim to this, which made the accumulator deeply unpopular with the ladies of the house. It was usually the men of the house, however, who attended to the changing of it when it needed to be charged or topped up with distilled water, so many a pair of dungarees, jackets, shirts or boiler suits were destroyed in the same way. So it was responsible for a good deal of domestic disharmony. However, listening to the radio itself had by that time become so popular with the family that most disputes were settled amicably.

Later the so-called all-dry radio became available. This used a single dry battery connected to the radio with a four-pin plug which could only be inserted one way. They were slightly more expensive to run, however, and old habits die hard so the accumulator, despite its inconvenience and revolting practices, remained in use for many years.

Portable radios, which all used dry batteries, also became popular, though users of them were sometimes a bit hazy about the principles involved. One man described seeing one demonstrated thus: "He switched it on then, he just opened the window about half an inch and it started playing loud and clear."

There were many competing makers of dry batteries, all claiming to give the longest life. Winner, Drydex, Vidor, Ray-O-Vac etc. For some years Willie and his friend, Angus Hoseason, had had their own small business making dry batteries. The batteries they produced were said to be very good but probably because the market – which was really only the inhabitants of Yell – was just too small, ultimately the business proved to be uneconomic and had to be abandoned.

Next came the transistor, but early transistor radios could not equal the performance of the valve sets. They were prone to excessive background noise and poor reproduction. It was to be the mid-1960s and with the introduction of the new FM band before they could compete. At about that time many young men worked at the Antarctic whaling where they met Norwegian whalers and were able to acquire Norwegian-built portables, which, whether valve or transistor, were for some strange reason much superior to the British-made variety.

Modern Inventions

Willie also became very interested in photography. He somehow acquired a box camera and took many photos with it. He did all his own developing and printing, using dishes and a home-made safety lamp as he was never able to afford a developing tank. He used a process which produced sepia prints but they seemed very prone to fading. He took many photos, some of which still survive, but unfortunately most of them have deteriorated to the extent that even with modern restoration techniques they could not be made good enough to reproduce here.

Like many Shetlanders of that time, older brother Donny was a versatile man. He had served in the navy during the First World War and in later years he carried out both radio and watch repairs. Once, during an emergency when he was at sea and they had somehow run out of bread, he also baked enough bread for the entire crew. He had bought a record called *Keep the Kettle Boiling Mary*, as a tribute to his girlfriend at the time, whose name was Mary. It was at that time possible to obtain blank records and put your own recordings on them by speaking or singing into the gramophone sound-box. Donny decided to try this and recruited one of his brothers to operate the gramophone while he performed the song.

He started off rather formally by announcing, "This is a demonstration of a song by John Williamson." Then he suddenly stopped as he realised he had forgotten what he was going to sing. Not just the name, but the whole thing. Presumably he had some signal arranged with his brother to stop the recording in an emergency, but if so, he must have forgotten that too. Instead he just yelled very loudly, "Stop!" Of course, this was recorded onto the blank disc, so if it really was meant to be a demonstration it was less than successful.

The discs were intended to be reusable and it was normally possible to record another programme which would remove the first one. But this time, perhaps because the "Stop!" was just too loud, it proved impossible to remove it. Other songs were recorded and played back successfully, but when it got back to the appropriate place, the "Stop!" was still very clearly audible.

Gramophones were prone to various faults and it was quite common for them to suffer from a broken spring, which had to be replaced. This was no easy task. There is considerable power stored in a wound-up spring and these springs were quite large. If one was not very careful the spring might suddenly discharge itself, the razor-sharp edges of the steel lashing out and cutting anything with which it came in contact. Nevertheless, several of the boys became competent at replacing the spring and were often employed to carry out the necessary work with none of them seeming to suffer any injury.

Someone once visited the workshop belonging to Willie and his friend Angus Hoseason, with a gramophone which needed a new spring fitted. Willie had become very experienced in this job but on this occasion Angus was keen to try his hand at it. Willie tried to persuade him not to attempt it, and explained that not only was it difficult, it could be painful, or even dangerous. The spring had to be held very tightly and the sharp edges were inclined to cut painfully into the fingers. And, as mentioned, it was essential not to release it and let it unwind suddenly to lash out with great force, which could also cause very nasty cuts. Angus was still determined to try it but became so stressed that he asked Willie for a glass of water. Willie obliged, but soon Angus was in so much trouble that Willie had to take over and complete the job himself.

There was a remarkable man called Willie Arthur who lived in West Yell. He had lost one hand in an accident with a shotgun and had fitted an empty tin to his motorbike handlebars so that he could put the stump of his hand into it, which enabled him to ride his bike as before. He also somehow managed to carry out this gramophone spring repair quite regularly. Willie, my father, could never understand how he accomplished it: "When I do it I need both hands, and would certainly prefer to have a third," he said.

The Film Guild

After the war ended, Willie and his family returned to Yell. He obtained a job with the Highlands and Islands Film Guild, giving film shows in the local halls. After a conference of local authorities and other interested parties held in Edinburgh in 1946, the Film Guild had been formed with the aim of providing a fleet of mobile 16mm cinema units to cover outlying districts, both on the mainland and in the islands.

As well as the evening entertainment shows they also showed educational films for schoolchildren, which brought in some money from the education authorities. This was quite straightforward if they could be shown in the halls, but could be decidedly awkward if they had to be shown in the schools which were often not very suitable for the purpose, with makeshift blackouts and other modifications having to be devised.

The first mobile unit was established on the Shetland Mainland, with George Horne as operator, in 1947. Later units followed both in the islands and remote parts of the Scottish Highlands. Soon mobile units had been established in Sutherland, Argyll, Inverness, Ross and Cromarty and Orkney.

In the late 1940s it had been decided to establish a unit in the Shetland North Isles. Willie had applied for the operator's job and had been successful. A 25-cwt Commer van was provided for transport in Yell. The van had to be quite long to hold the screen, which was about 2m long, and it also held a small J.A.P. petrol generator to provide electrical power for the projection equipment, there being no mains power in Yell at that time.

He gave his first show, *The Sea Hawk* starring Errol Flynn, in the Mid Yell Hall on 3rd April, 1950. It was a great success, with quite a large audience who seemed to have enjoyed it. Of course the halls, being multi-purpose buildings, varied greatly in their suitability for film shows. In Yell the best was Burravoe. For a start it was the only one that had adequate heating – provided by large, green paraffin heaters – and it was long,

narrow and had a rather low ceiling which helped to contain the heat and gave it good acoustics. The downside was that almost everyone smoked in those days so that by the time the film ended you were only seeing it through a blue haze. Later, the hall was made even better by adding a projection room. This was done by cutting holes in the wall of the men's cloakroom which was at one end of the hall. Four holes – two for the projector beams and two more to allow the projectionist to see through and align and focus the projectors – were needed. This greatly reduced the noise of the projectors, so indirectly improved the sound. Another convenient feature for the projectionist was that the hall had an adjacent car park which meant that the equipment did not have to be carried very far and the van could be left there during the show.

From the projectionist's point of view, Cullivoe was the most inconvenient hall. It usually wasn't possible to get the van anywhere near the hall. Instead it had to be left on the main road and all the equipment carried by hand up a very steep path. In dry weather it was sometimes possible to reverse part of the way up this path, but the van could not be left there during the performance as the generator would be standing at too much of an angle, which could damage it, so the van had to be taken back and parked on the main road. At first Willie left it heading into the wind so that the back doors could be left open to cool the generator without admitting rain, or even snow, but in time the local policeman pointed out that it was illegal to park in darkness on the wrong side of the road so it was then necessary to open either a window or one door, or even tie the doors partly shut, depending on the weather. Another problem was that with side lamps being switched on for an extended period the van battery would become discharged. Willie solved this one by connecting a battery charger to the generator power supply.

The only heating in the Cullivoe hall was a single Tilley radiator, which in a large hall was almost useless. The main door into the hall faced west and was in poor condition so a cold wind blew in almost constantly in winter, while in summer the rays of the setting sun shone through onto the screen. This was cured by literally papering over the cracks. Nevertheless, there was a large and loyal group of film fans in Cullivoe who were prepared to brave the elements so attendances were usually quite good. On a winter's night it was hard to believe, but with a large crowd on a warm summer's night the hall could become uncomfortably warm. This rarely happened at film shows, but at weddings or regatta concerts it was not unusual, so a ventilator had been fitted. There was no quick and easy way of controlling it. A young, fit and preferably rather small person had to climb into the loft using a ladder, then scramble up into the rafters to reach the ventilator and turn it off or on. Because it was so awkward to use, it became common practice to leave it open all summer then close it at the start of the winter. It was not an easy task but Gordon Jamieson, a keen film fan and talented accordionist, who later wrote a book on the buses of Shetland, performed it regularly for years.

It was also in Cullivoe that the famous incident occurred when a cow, placidly grazing in the evening twilight, absentmindedly chewed through the power supply cable from the generator. Fortunately, for both the cow and the film show, it happened after the generator had been stopped.

Heavy snow was a very common problem and on one occasion Willie was stranded in Cullivoe for a week before having to come home on the *Earl of Zetland*. Getting aboard was rather a frightening experience. In pitch darkness a rope with a loop at one end was lowered from a crane. Willie was told to put one foot into the loop and take a firm hold of the rope, the crane would then lift him up and lower him on to the deck of the ship. Scary enough for a fit person but for Willie, who really only had full control of one leg, it must have been terrifying. However, it was successful. Another week was to pass before the roads had been cleared enough for him to return to Cullivoe and drive the van home.

With the job being for the North Isles, it meant that Willie also had to provide shows in the neighbouring isles of Unst and Fetlar. There were no car ferries in those days so all the equipment had to be taken on the small ferry boats already in use. Local taxi services were then employed to transport Willie and the equipment to the halls. If the state of the tide was unsuitable, ladders had to be used to get the equipment on and off the boats.

At that time there was no regular service using small boats to Fetlar so transport there and back had to be arranged using the regular visits of the much larger *Earl*. This meant using a flitboat, which was very awkward as it meant that the equipment, which was not particularly light, had in effect to be transferred three times: firstly from the Mid Yell pier to the *Earl*, then from the *Earl* to the flitboat, and finally from the flitboat to the Fetlar pier. There were two projectors, weighing about 25kg each, a 110V transformer about the same, and a large box containing cables, spools, spare lamps etc added another 25kg. Then there were the speakers and projector stands, lighter but in a more awkward shape.

In the early days there was no mains power in Unst or Fetlar so generators had to be installed at the halls in use there. In Unst, Baltasound and Haroldswick used identical generators, single-cylinder air-cooled ones made by Petter. They were very reliable though a bit noisy. Uyeasound used a four-cylinder water-cooled engine which was also very reliable and less noisy. In 1953 admission charges were for 2/- (2 shillings) for adults, and 9d (9 pence) for children.

In practice Willie spent three days in the fortnight in Unst, giving shows in Baltasound, Uyeasound and Haroldswick, and one overnight stop for the one location in Fetlar. As if this was not enough he sometimes showed religious films for the church. Sometimes these were shown in the actual churches, which were often not very suitable for this purpose. The tall, narrow windows had to be fitted with blackouts. The seats were permanently set in place and there was often only one door, so the projectionist was very limited as to where to place the equipment. In one, erecting the screen involved climbing precariously on top of the pulpit, which to make matters worse had padded armrests. In another, the local minister in his robe became entangled in the record player table. However, these shows were very popular and always drew a large crowd despite having the same heating problems as the village halls.

It was in Fetlar that he once became involved in a nasty accident, when the car in which he was a passenger lost its steering control. It went off the road into the ditch and came to an abrupt halt. Among the luggage aboard was a metal box containing two large and very heavy 110V transformers. It was thrown forward by the impact and would certainly have hit the passenger in the front seat had it not been for Willie's quick reaction of thrusting his hand in front of it. The blow he received caused him a broken rib, but undoubtedly saved the passenger from serious injury, or worse.

After that the system used in Fetlar was changed. It became what was called a static unit. A projector, generator, and some other equipment was permanently installed in Fetlar and a local man was recruited as operator. A copy of the film currently being shown on the circuit was sent to the Fetlar operator and Willie did not have to visit the island at all. He was relieved about this as Fetlar could be a place which was often isolated by stormy conditions.

In theory Willie's job did not involve repairs or maintenance of either vehicles or equipment. This was intended to be provided by the Guild's technical officer, Jack Orviss. He was based in Inverness, however, so although he made periodic visits to all the units and checked all their equipment religiously – even dismantling the projectors down to individual ball races, and even sometimes dismantling the ball races themselves – with the aim of making everything as reliable as was humanly possible, it was inevitable that Willie would become involved in breakdowns from time to time. He was extremely good at carrying out repairs and acquired such a reputation that Jack himself advised one of the relief operators, who travelled around all the units to fill in for regular operators who were on holiday, that if he experienced any technical trouble when he was in Shetland he should contact Willie.

In 1956 Willie suffered a serious illness. Although he made a good recovery he was never again fit for heavy work and had to resign from the Film Guild. Nevertheless, such was his reputation that he was sometimes consulted when difficult problems cropped up. One such occurred when the Fetlar unit, after working very successfully for several years, suddenly began to burn out an excessive number of projector lamps. Willie agreed to visit the scene and asked me to come with him. It was not obvious whether the trouble was with the generator engine or the associated circuitry. Willie decided to concentrate on the engine, which he was convinced was using too rich a mixture, while I investigated the electrics. Willie started to adjust the mixture screw, paying no attention to someone who advised him to leave it as it was as that was where it worked best. Soon Willie had it running much more smoothly. I found faults in the electrical installation too, but I forget what they were. However, when all had been repaired, the installation worked perfectly with no excessive projector lamp mortality, and gave no further trouble, right up to the final show in 1970.

By 1954 a quarter of a million attendances were recorded at Film Guild showings, but by 1960 this had dropped to 220,000. And then came television. In 1957, TV had arrived in the Highlands and slowly but surely spread ever further north. In 1961 the Guild's mobile units were reduced from 14 to 12 by integrating two of the units operating in Inverness-shire into one, and three of the units in Argyllshire into two. Television reached Shetland in 1964, with results that were just as devastating to film audiences as they had been in other parts of the country. The mobile units were again reduced, from 12 to 11, by integrating the services in Sutherland and northwest Ross-shire from two units into one, and running the whole of Shetland as one unit. Unst, which had been in trouble even before the arrival of television, and was soon in severe difficulty as it had now got a mains power supply, was changed to a static unit with Harold Sutherland as operator. Of course, these problems caused by TV were not confined to Scotland, or even Britain as the film industry was in crisis world wide.

Many film producers saw widescreen films as the answer. Unfortunately this led to the familiar situation of a format war with Cinemascope, Vista Vision, Cinerama and others competing. Unfortunately for the Guild, one major film renter advised them that films in the old 1.33 ratio would soon cease to be produced so they invested considerable expense in screens and projection lenses suitable for showing the more modern style. However, it soon became obvious that this prediction was going to be no more accurate than this kind of crystal gazing usually is, and films continued to come in many different sizes and formats. The new screens were cumbersome in use and, in the end, most of them suffered the indignity of being adjusted to the old 1.33 aspect ratio and were left permanently erected in some of the more remote halls.

At about the same time the showing of trailers for forthcoming films was abandoned as an economy measure, but this removed an important link between one film and the next and I personally always considered it a mistake. However, by that time most schools had obtained their own projectors so the Guild's educational shows were discontinued, with a consequent loss of income. When the time came that almost all the halls had mains power installed, the Guild decided that wherever possible permanent screens would be fitted in the halls. This meant the large vans were no longer needed and they were replaced by Austin A35s.

The Film Guild tried many modernisations to try to make their shows more attractive, including the fashionable wide screens which proved not particularly popular. More successful were the drapes – dark blue curtains – which surrounded the screen at both sides and below; these seemed to improve the contrast and were popular. Willie made an excellent set of footlights which could be easily folded for transport, but the business of setting up the associated cable, plugs and dimmer resistance was tiresome so they were eventually considered more trouble than they were worth and were discontinued. They tried more modern projectors with improved lighting and slightly improved sound but with some disadvantages, such as slightly more mechanical noise and the more serious issue of projection lamps which sometimes exploded. These explosions were not just a slight pop, but with a noise almost like a gunshot, and a thick cloud of dust, the shattered remnants of the lamp were blown high in the air by the cooling fan to descend on anything in the way.

But on a winter night it was going to be very difficult to overcome the attraction of watching TV in a warm, comfortable room. The population of this whole area was already in decline and although the Guild fought hard to maintain their services, and even to expand in some areas, audiences continued to decline.

In 1970 the Film Guild, despite all the efforts that had been made to preserve it, had to yield to the inevitable and finally closed. One national newspaper announced the closure by saying that there would now be no more buccaneering film showmen to be seen on the roads, which made it seem a lot more exciting than it actually was. I somehow doubt if many of these hard-working men ever thought of themselves in such glamorous terms.

More on the Film Guild

Readers from outside the Highlands and Islands of Scotland may not understand the references to the rural film shows provided by the

Highlands & Islands Film Guild. I will describe a typical show in Yell in the 1950s. In the early days the projectionist would go out to start the generator, which was fitted in a 25-cwt Commer van, about 15 minutes before the start time of the show. It was a J.A.P. petrol-powered engine and had to be started by hand. When he had got it going he would return to the hall and play records until it was time to start the film. The player could play only 78 rpm records and used old-fashioned gramophone needles, so seemed even then to be a bit ancient and the needles, being obsolete, could be difficult to obtain. However, a decidedly eccentric lady, who lived alone in North-a-Voe with an army of cats, had a part-time business supplying gramophone spares. She was also a keen film-goer so was more than happy to help.

Later the old record player was replaced with a more modern one which could play 45 rpm and 33 rpm discs and younger members of the audience started to bring along some of their own discs, which made a very varied programme. One favourite was *Sloop John B* by the Beach Boys, another was *Come Down the Mountain Katy Daly* – I forget who performed this one. From the projectionist's point of view the great advantage of these records was that they were much lighter than the very heavy 78 rpm type.

Breakdowns were relatively rare and were mostly caused by broken wires at plug connections, due to the number of times they were connected and disconnected. Usually these were discovered before the film started and were easily repaired, though the situation was not helped by one rather panicky caretaker who used to say, "Another half hour and the people will be coming."

In the meantime a crowd of customers, mostly children and young people, sometimes carrying their chosen records, would have gathered, pressing the projectionist with questions about the film and the supporting programme. At last the magic moment would arrive. Someone removed the Tilley lamp and the show started.

Two projectors were used to provide a continuous performance, and it was a practical necessity to begin with the trailer for the next film, as these were usually too short to allow time to thread up the second projector. There was always a British Pathé newsreel, often a cartoon – *Popeye*, *Tom*

& Jerry, *Bugs Bunny* etc – and sometimes a more serious documentary. Some of these were a little bizarre, such as the one which instructed us quite seriously on how to stoke the boiler on an old-style steam train. The instructor kept repeating himself, to make sure we got the message: "Remember the golden rule. Little and often." When he then said, "Now let us run through the method once more," the audience's response was of uproarious laughter. Another gave instructions on how to diagnose and treat foot rot in sheep, which may have been of interest to the crofting community.

There were also advertisements: "Never go without a Capstan" for cigarettes; and ones for Cadbury's Roses chocolates, the Bank of Scotland, a light tractor made by David Brown and, even more strange, the ill-fated Princess flying boat. Then at last came the main feature. With the show now well under way pipes and cigarettes were lit and a blue haze began to form. Often the distinctive aroma of Russian cigarettes could be prominent.

Films in those days were much less violent than they are today but in the era of Alfred Hitchcock they could still be tense and scary. One lady dropped her glasses on the floor at a tense moment and caused a chorus of screams from the girls in the audience. The projectors used spring steel belts which occasionally broke and shot out, striking the wall behind with some force, which could also sometimes cause panic. Usually when this happened the projectionist would turn the take-up spool by hand until the spool came to an end, which avoided making an unnecessary stop, which was always best avoided.

When a spool was coming to an end the projectionist watched the top right-hand corner of the screen looking for the change-over marks. There were two of these spaced a few seconds apart; they lasted only 1/6th of a second but were clearly visible if you were looking for them. If the change was done well, all the audience would notice was a slight increase in projector noise while both motors were running. If the films had been threaded in the approved manner the second projector motor was switched on when the first mark appeared, then at the second mark the picture and sound was switched across. A special change-over box with switches, cables and plugs was connected to the projectors and made this quite easy. Unfortunately, the change-over marks were not entirely reliable: sometimes there was only one, or sometimes none at all. If you were caught out you might switch the lamp and sound across too early, causing the series of numbers to appear on the screen, which was met with hoots of derision from the younger members of the audience. It was safer the first time you showed the picture to thread the film with the starting frame about to enter the gate, where it would be projected instantly. Then, if the change-over marks were missing or misplaced, the film could be started by switching on the second projector motor, followed immediately by the lamp and sound change-over switch. With care, quite a neat change-over could be done in this way.

Another thing which could cause panic was the switchboard box, which was where the generator power supply was plugged in. These contained what were called charging mats: electric heating elements woven into a sort of asbestos fabric. In damp weather moisture could condense on these and when the generator was started it would produce steam that looked like billows of smoke, causing shouts of "Fire!" and a rush to the door to tell the projectionist, who would be out starting one generator to stop the other generator as the equipment had gone on fire. This type of weather was also unpopular with the projectionist as it could cause the metal switches to become live, causing a nasty shock when they were touched. This was particularly troublesome when Willie was using his cement mixer as cement causes a drying effect on the hands and has the result of making the skin very sensitive to shocks. The fundamental cause of this was that the old J.A.P. generator had no proper earthing system. When the system was modernised by a diesel-powered generator with a stabilised voltage regulator fitted most of them disappeared.

At the end of every show a short piece of film showed the Queen and Buckingham Palace while the national anthem was played. The audience stood up or ran for the door, according to taste, and the show was over. Then it was time to check the takings to see if they corresponded with the tickets sold, after which everyone, including the projectionist, dispersed to wend their way homeward. These shows were very popular, especially with children and young people, and provided much needed entertainment before the arrival of TV which rendered them largely obsolete. But, unlike TV, the event was a social occasion where friends met and conversed before the show started. Even today there are still people alive who remember them with great affection.

The Tilley Lamp

In the days before mains power almost all village halls used Tilley lamps for lighting. These were a great improvement on the wick paraffin lamps which preceded them, which gave little more light than a candle. The Tilley lamp gave about as much light as a 100W bulb. The reason for this was that instead of burning the paraffin in liquid form, it was heated to produce a vapour which burned much more efficiently.

Lighting it was, however, a rather complex business. It had to be preheated using a device called a torch – a clip-on gadget with asbestos wicks which had to be soaked in methylated spirit – then clipped on to a metal tube (termed the vaporiser) where paraffin was changed to vapour.

Except in very cold conditions, by the time the flame from the meths had burned low the lamp was ready to be lit. This was done by lifting the torch up so that what flame was left was just below the burner, then gently pumping some air into the tank. If all went well the vapour would light, the torch could be removed, and more air was pumped into the tank to produce a decent light.

The paraffin tank, normally called the fountain, usually had a built-in hand-powered air pump which was used to provide pressure to force the paraffin up through the vaporiser, where it would be turned into a vapour, then into the burner which contained jets which could then be lit. As the flame was non-luminous a flimsy mantle was attached to the burner and gave a very useful light. The process could not be hurried. If you pumped the air in too soon, non-vaporised paraffin would be forced into the burner and a highly dangerous sheet of flame would shoot out. It was a complex device which was prone to many troubles, but still a very effective method of lighting. Like any other device which used naked flames it had to be treated with respect.

Once at a film show, after the Tilley had been removed when the show started, the hall caretaker became worried about where it might have been placed and went to check. It was as well that he did as the helper had taken it into the hall kitchen and set it on a cabinet without noticing that it was directly under a shelf. Even when working correctly a Tilley lamp emitted very hot gas. By the time the caretaker found it the underside of the shelf was too hot to touch.

In most of the stories about motor repairs the Tilley lamp would have been used for lighting as it was the only sufficiently strong light available. It was far from ideal, as the light could not be easily directed and you had to be very careful not to get your head directly above it as the hot gas could cause scorched eyebrows or worse. For this reason it often had to be supplemented by a battery-powered flashlight. These came in various types and sizes. Two of the most common were the twin-cell, for use as a bicycle headlamp but which could be easily detached for hand-held use; and the huge five-cell torch which, with 7.5v of battery and a large reflector was very powerful, but inconvenient for use in a confined space.

One of the weak spots of the Tilley lamp was that the mantle glowed white hot when in use. As in the well-known analogy of the moth and flame, it attracted flying insects such as large moths and bluebottles which quite often flew into it, with fatal results both for insect and mantle.

Some models had the mantle surrounded by a glass globe, which was effective but made the lighting process even more awkward. Another trouble spot was the vaporiser. The hole through which the vapour exited it was tiny and often became blocked. A knob could be turned which briefly inserted a needle into the hole to clear it. This usually worked but there was always a risk that the point might break off, blocking the hole permanently, which meant a new vaporiser.

A variation was the Tilley radiator which was designed more for heat rather than light. It used a more robust mantle which only glowed red hot and rarely gave trouble, and had a polished metal reflector to point the heat in the right direction. It was very reliable but the heat it produced was very local and little use in the halls of that time, except sometimes in some of the ante rooms such as cloakrooms or club rooms.

If the main hall had to be heated, large but portable paraffin heaters were available and were more effective. They were not without their problems either, however. The top part was hinged and it could be bent over to access the wick. On at least occasion someone lifted the heater by the handle to move it, but the hinge opened and the tank with burning wick attached fell out onto the wooden floor. Prompt action by one of the young men present prevented the fire spreading.

The Cement Mixer

While working for the Film Guild, Willie had acquired a Morris 8 car for his personal use and decided to build his own house in the village of North-a-Voe, where his wife Tamar Mann had been born and where most of his in-laws lived. Before he started on the house he designed and built a wind-powered cement mixer to use in its construction. The modern craze for renewable energy and recycling are nothing new to Shetlanders of times past. For generations they were used, not from a desire to appear environmentally friendly but from sheer necessity.

When Willie decided to build his house of mass concrete he was immediately faced with a problem: how was the required amount of concrete to be mixed? The standard method used at that time involved two men with shovels, working as a team on a board. It was hard work, needed considerable skill and, worst of all, was painfully slow. In Yell, long before the days of piped water and mains electricity, and given the financial constraints of the period, buying a power-driven mixer was out of the question. So, like generations before, Willie turned to the wind as a power source and devised what today would be called the turbine – an eight-bladed windmill that drove the mixer drum via a reduction gear provided by pulleys and a belt drive.

As Willie was still working for the Guild it meant spending three days in the fortnight in Unst, so he made a virtue of necessity by taking his materials and tools to Unst with him and was able to work on his project in the Springfield garage until it was time to set off for the show in the evening. As a bonus, he often met his brother, Henry, who also visited Unst regularly to teach navigation and seamanship in the schools. Some years later the Springfield garage, which also housed the petrol-driven Stuart Turner generator used for lighting the hotel before the arrival of mains power to Unst, was destroyed by fire, but Willie's project had been completed long before then.

A cement mixer drum has to turn slowly. If it is run too fast the contents become pressed to the sides by centrifugal force and no mixing takes place. For this reason, and also to prevent the mixer reaching a dangerous speed, when the contents were emptied out some form of governor was needed. In the system designed by Willie, an arrangement of weights and springs was connected to the individual turbine blades. When the turbine reached its design speed, the weights were thrown outwards and turned the blades into the feathered position. In practice this worked very well. If a shovelful of chips was thrown into the drum when it was running light at full speed the clatter of the weights falling back to the optimum position was clearly audible, to be followed seconds later by silence as the rotor started to pick up speed and throw the weights out once more.

Originally four blades were used but this proved insufficient so four more were added. It proved unnecessary to fit the governing system to the extra four blades as the air braking effect of the other feathered blades was enough to control the turbine speed. In this configuration it was very successful and allowed mixing to be carried out in almost any wind conditions. In the event of complete loss of wind, mixing could still be carried out by inserting a shovel behind one of the paddles inside the drum and turning it by hand; while much slower than when power driven, it was still faster and lighter work than the old shovel and mixing-board system.

As always in those days, lack of funds meant that as much as possible of Willie's machine would be made from recycled materials or, as it would have been called in those days, junk. The blades were made from old corrugated iron hammered flat and the governor weights were cut from an old lead pipe. The governor springs were cut from an old car inner tube, the blades were attached to a bicycle wheel, and the drive belt was a piece of rope spliced into an endless loop. The drum was made from a barrel, bolted to a motorcycle wheel, which also served as the driven pulley and provided the drum bearing. The fork mount was made from a scrapped car chassis. Almost all the rest was made from scrap pieces of wood or metal. The only parts bought new were the blade hinges and some of the bolts which held it all together.

The weak spot was, of course, that there was no convenient means of turning the turbine round in the event of the wind direction changing. Willie considered a variety of ideas but never came up with any that he considered worth further testing. A major snag with all these ideas was that the ground on which it would stand was by no means smooth or level. Levelling it in those days when no power machinery was available and the only tools available were the pick and shovel together with a good deal of expensive labour, was not really a viable option. In practice the inability to follow the changes of wind direction was not such a severe disadvantage as might be thought. There was sufficient surplus of power to allow mixing to continue even with the wind direction a considerable distance from the optimum. The whole set-up could, if needed, be turned manually to face in a different direction but this was very time consuming and was rarely resorted to. Later, Willie's brother Hughie also built a cement mixer, loosely based on Willie's design, but he had a tractor and used its PTO (power take-off) to power it.

The Inventor

A reputation can be a two-edged sword. There can be a downside to it, and one time Willie was once approached by a man who was convinced he had solved the problem of perpetual motion. Though a skilled carpenter and boat builder he did not have the mechanical skills in metal work needed to build a prototype, but he was sure Willie could do it.

So many weird and wonderful contraptions have been built, and are still being built, by imaginative people who have failed to understand the principles involved, that the idea is probably not original, and that it's likely someone has earlier tried out a similar machine.

The inventor's idea really consisted of a compressed air engine which drove an air pump which would pump up the tank which drove the engine. There are many similar ideas, such as the electric motor which drives a generator which provides power to the motor. They all fail because they require both machines to be 100 per cent efficient, which in practice they can never be. Even if it was achieved it would still only be a scientific curiosity as no power could have been extracted from it.

But the man was convinced that it was perfectly possible and when it was completed and revealed to an astonished world, Willie and the inventor would share the enormous profits the machine would make. Willie, however, knew enough about the principles involved to recognise the impossibility of the system and was unwilling to spend time on a project which he knew could not possibly succeed. Convincing the inventor, however, was another matter and it all ended in a long and fruitless argument which dragged on for weeks and which Willie found very trying.

Willie had a converted hut which he had purchased after the war and used as a workshop. The inventor came to haunt it and plague and distract Willie from more important work. He was sure that the secret of success was in using a sufficiently large flywheel, and he was unconvinced with Willie's argument: that a larger flywheel would require more power to get it moving, it could only store power not create it, and so would not help. Neither was he much impressed by Willie's very successful cement mixer. He always insisted that it never mixed the ingredients as thoroughly as could be done by the two men with shovels system which was, quite frankly, nonsense.

Neither side managed to convince the other so the dispute was not ended until the inventor died. I am sure he never forgave Willie for turning down the opportunity of fame and fortune for both of them.

Entertainment

Long before the arrival of the Highlands and Islands Film Guild there was locally-organised entertainment in the islands. Dances were one of the most common forms and for dancing one needed music, and a family as musically gifted as the Williamsons was bound to become very involved with the entertainment scene.

Like most men of his generation, Willie Snr had spent a great deal of his early life as a merchant seaman. At one time he had been shipmates with two men who, like himself, could play the fiddle. They decided to buy a fiddle between them to provide entertainment. They also agreed that whichever one of them was last to leave the ship would, in effect, fall heir

KARI W.

to it and would take it home with him. As it happened, Willie Snr was the last to leave when he retired from the sea so he acquired the fiddle and played it for many years, as well as teaching his sons to play.

There was an apocryphal story in the family about a wedding where only one fiddler could be obtained and he could only play one tune. It seems unlikely, but Willie Jnr once did have a rather similar experience. Of course he could play more than one tune but, unusually – for many men in Shetland at that time could play the fiddle – no-one could be found to relieve him during a prolonged dancing session. There is a theory that the phrase 'as fit as a fiddle' dates from the time when a solo fiddler would provide all the music for a wedding celebration; a feat of endurance. On this occasion, Willie had to continue until he became so tired that suddenly the bow fell out of his hand, proving that he was unfortunately not as fit as a fiddle.

A popular dance at that time was the eightsome reel and Willie was surprised when he started to play at dances that only one tune (I think it was the Scottish dance tune *Mrs Mcleod*) was ever used for it, although many others were quite suitable. Playing one tune over and over again is very boring and tiring for the performer. Anyone who has had the misfortune of having to perform endless re-runs of *The Grand Old Duke of York* on any instrument, or even a gramophone or record player, at children's parties will be well aware of this.

Willie tried using other suitable tunes but the dancers just looked at him, like Cortez's men in Keats' poem *A Wild Surmise*, and made no attempt to start the dance. Willie's next attempt was more successful. After getting them started by playing the obligatory *Mrs Mcleod* he changed into another tune which he knew was quite suitable, then he was able to change again. If the dancers ever noticed anything they never complained.

Later the fiddle came to be accompanied, and sometimes replaced, by the piano-accordion which was usually louder and could sound really well. In skilled hands the sound of the fiddle and accordion together is very pleasant. Many of the old Scottish and Irish tunes were still used for dancing, but after the war many young men were employed by the Norwegian whaling fleet and made regular trips to South Georgia where they met Norwegian accordion players who taught them tunes from Norway and the Norwegian style of playing, which is quite different from the Scottish. These tunes became very popular. One called the *M.T.B. Waltz* was named after the motor torpedo boats which were very much in action around Shetland during the Second World War. *Life in the Finland Woods* was another favourite.

At about the same time the coming of radio brought in American and Canadian tunes which were also very popular, particularly with singers. The old American West always weaves a strange fascination so it's no surprise that the strains of *Springtime in the Rockies* or *Back in the Saddle Again* became very familiar in the halls of Yell, though many of their listeners had never seen the Rockies or been in any saddle other than a motorbike's.

In general, someone who can play the fiddle can also sing, though they may not have a good voice. All the Williamson family did sing, and at one time Willie sang bass in the church choir. His sister Anderina also sang and was one of those who battled unsuccessfully to compete with Donny's "Stop!" For the most part however, the boys preferred the fiddle, particularly Willie and Hughie who had a duet act with fiddles which they performed in many churches, playing hymns and sacred songs with Willie playing the air and Hughie the accompaniment.

As well as the dances there were many concerts where local people could display their talent, which in many cases was considerable. There were many good singers around at that time. On one memorable occasion Willie's brother George, fully dressed and made up for the part, gave a stirring performance of *The Spaniard Who Blighted My Life*.

Local concerts often included what was called a sketch. This was a short, one-act play of humorous content, often written locally in Shetland dialect. Kari became a very popular author of these, with *Tammie's Proposal* and *Kirstie's Quandary* being memorable. Her uncle, Johnny Mann, was also prominent, both as writer and performer. Another prominent writer was Angus Hoseason, but some people thought that his solo efforts were maybe not so good as those he wrote in collaboration with Johnny.

Sometimes a group from one village would form a concert party and put on performances in other halls, but sometimes this did not go exactly to plan. One time a party from North-a-Voe hit a snag when they discovered that the piano in the hall they were visiting was out of tune. Fortunately, Willie's versatility saved the day and he managed to retune it well enough to enable the performances to go ahead.

Some of the concerts advertised could not be performed today. Smoking concerts – whatever they were – seem unlikely to be approved, and neither would the one (I dare not mention what it was called) that was a sort of minstrel show and involved performing in black face. On the other hand, sacred concerts with hymns and religious songs were popular with the large church-going contingent.

The Williamson family were all very musical and their father and all his sons played the fiddle. Unfortunately, some years before, Willie had suffered that fiddler's nightmare and an occupational hazard of pioneer motorists, a broken wrist. He was working on the Shetland Mainland at the time and at a remote spot in the north of that island when it happened. This meant he had to drive all the way back to Lerwick, about 30 miles, to get medical attention, which must have been very painful. In time, however, he made a good recovery and did, quite literally, play the violin again. Although he was still considered by his audiences to be a fine performer he always thought that he was never quite so good afterwards.

Coronation Day

Among the events planned in Yell to celebrate Coronation Day 1953 was a procession of floats and decorated vehicles. One of the most ambitious of these projects was the one undertaken by a group of young North-a-Voe men. Mounted on a V8 truck borrowed from Karl Anderson of Mid Yell, it was intended to represent a log cabin and was built from old cardboard boxes on a wooden frame. The truck was parked in the playground of the North-a-Voe school and all the conversion work took place there. The cabin enclosed the whole of the bonnet and driving cab, the boxes being painted to give the appearance of the log cabin.

The open back of the truck was also covered in boxes and painted to represent a walled enclosure. This part held the performers – Graham

Smith and Willie Nicholson played fiddle and accordion while Arthur Nicholson and Muir Williamson sang cowboy songs, and Muir also played the guitar – and all were appropriately dressed. The driver was Bobby Smith. At last Coronation Day dawned, overcast with a strong north wind, bitterly cold but mercifully dry. Rain would have caused problems for the musicians, and if it was heavy enough might even have caused the cardboard boxes to disintegrate. The whole structure proved just about driveable, though the driver's view was very restricted, and the walls of the cabin considerably reduced the steering lock available, making it difficult to negotiate corners.

There was no policeman stationed in Yell at that time so there was, as the cowboys might have said, "No law west of Dodge," or in this case north of Yell Sound. However, there was a last-minute hitch which could have threatened the whole project. Someone reported to Karl that they had seen a policeman in Mid Yell. This was quite possible as sometimes, on special occasions such as regattas, one was sent up to Yell from Lerwick, causing consternation among the owners of motorcycles as many of the cycles were not licensed. Karl spoke to Bobby about this, pointing out that apart from its other failings the number plates on the contraption could not be seen, making it very obviously illegal. However, someone else turned up and was able to explain the sighting. Lowrie Brown of Mid Yell had got a policeman's uniform which he had put on and wandered around in as a highly illegal joke. The procession went ahead as planned and was a complete success, although the musicians certainly suffered from the cold. What all this had to do with the Coronation is unclear but, of course, the Queen was head of the Commonwealth and the log cabin might have been Canadian.

Cousin Jimmy

Many of Willie's in-laws lived in North-a-Voe and as a family they seem to have had more than their share of colourful characters. One of the most memorable characters was Tamar's second cousin, Jimmy. I have given him a degree of anonymity by omitting his surname, but I think anyone who knew him will have no trouble identifying him. He was almost the same age as Tamar and was tall and strongly built, with thick wiry hair that stood up in all directions, rather like a young Patrick Moore. He never lost his hair, although in later years it went completely white so that when he was well dressed he looked quite distinguished. He was what would nowadays be called a workaholic. He worked all the hours that God sent, flat out all the time. This was not caused by greed, as some people thought, for he worked just as hard when he was working for an employer.

When he was not working he was speaking, and he spoke the same way as he worked – fast, hard and non-stop. The longer he spoke the more far-fetched his stories got. When he was coming to a particularly unbelievable part he would pause and say, "Telling you not one word of a lie, ... ". One tale was about a dog he once had that was always hiding from him. "Telling you not one word of a lie," and, pointing to a small torch on the dresser, "he could hide behind that flashlight!"

Jimmy had worked on a motorboat as a young man. "Telling you not one word of a lie, there were spiders in her as big as my fist," and he held out a clenched fist to demonstrate. Another story was about someone who always seemed to have plenty of money. According to Jimmy this was because "he worked in a bank and they all just helped themselves".

My favourite was one he told at my aunt Joan's. It was about someone who had died fairly young. "What did he die of?" Aunt Joan asked Jimmy.

"Leprosy."

Aunt Joan dropped her knitting and looked at him over her glasses. "Where did the boy get leprosy?"

Jimmy was never stuck for an answer. "Out of a leopard skin," he said.

He was impatient, quick tempered and assertive, but behind the bluster there was a very kind and generous nature. It was easy to fall out with Jimmy, but not so easy to be on bad terms with him for very long for he was never spiteful and the kindly side of him soon came to the surface again. He had no patience with bureaucracy and anything in the line of injustice infuriated him, and it was not just when he was personally involved. I remember him getting particularly angry on the subject of how little was done for disabled ex-servicemen after the war.

It was not to be expected that the rating officers would get a friendly

KARI W

welcome when they came to assess his house. "Who sent you here?" he demanded. "Where are you from?"

"We're from the county assessor," he was told.

"The county assessor," Jimmy interrupted, "you mean the county oppressor!"

One night that always sticks in my mind was the time our chimney went on fire. It was typical of Jimmy that he was one of the first to arrive to help, armed with a bag of salt. When we had managed to put the fire out he asked if he could use the phone. Like most people at that time he did not have a phone at his house and he wanted to speak to a local businessman. Jimmy had no children of his own but he had a nephew that he doted on, far too much really for the boy's own good. This nephew had bought a car from the businessman then found that the car had a number of faults, so he thought he had paid too much for it. Jimmy was going to take him to task about this.

There was none of this business of putting your complaint firmly but politely with Jimmy. When he had a dispute it was total war and he sailed in with all guns blazing. The family and those who had come to help with the fire did not, of course, deliberately listen, but unless you went outside the house you could not help hearing. Someone said that although we had managed to put out one fire we would soon have another for the very telephone wires would soon burst into flames with what was going over them!

Jimmy did not believe in this nonsense about not getting personal either. The businessman's father had owned a shop, which gave Jimmy an excuse for one of his most memorable lines: "Your father was a rogue, too, but he was an honest rogue."

Jimmy sometimes did make this kind of fine distinction. On another occasion he said, "It's not the scamps that cause the trouble, it's the rascals."

Whether there really was anything wrong with the car, or whether the verbal blitzkrieg just wore him down, in the end the businessman agreed to give Jimmy the refund he wanted.

Jimmy usually did win his cases. He was well into his seventies when Shetland Islands Council built some houses on his land and there was some dispute about the fence. The clerk of works came up from Lerwick to see him about it. "Come with me," he said to the foreman, "we'll go and sort out this old so and so."

The foreman said nothing. He knew Jimmy and had a pretty good idea who would sort out who. Ten minutes after they came to the house Jimmy had been given everything he wanted. Then he poured them out a dram.

Jimmy was not a teetotaller but he had a low opinion of drink and drinkers. Once he had to call the doctor to someone in the house. When the doctor had finished with the patient, and as it was close to Christmas, Jimmy poured him out a drink. "No, thank you, Jimmy," the doctor said, "I'd rather not if you don't mind."

"Oh, go on," Jimmy said, "it's Christmas, and I've poured it out now."

"No, really, Jimmy, I'm on duty and I'm not supposed to. You drink it yourself."

"I'm not drinking that," Jimmy said, "that's bloody poison, that is!"

Jimmy lived into the second half of his eighties and although he eventually slowed down, he was always able to work around and do his own turn. His mind was clear right to the end and he always took an interest in what was happening in the outside world. The last time I spoke to him was just after the Berlin Wall came down. As usual he came straight to the point: "Well, the Germans are all back together again. Will this mean another war?"

"Surely not, Jimmy," I said. "It's a different world now, things have changed a lot since those days."

"I hope you're right," he said, "it won't be in my time, of course, but I just wonder."

Not long after that, he was taking in his peats when he suddenly collapsed with a heart attack and a day or two later he was gone. I am sure it was the way he would have wanted to go. No prolonged period of illness and no bother to anybody. Jimmy had his faults, like the rest of us, but he had his good points too and when I think of him now it is always with affection, and even respect. He was a unique character and knowing him enriched my life. It would be a very dull world if we were all made the same.

Some Family Stories

The second eldest of the Williamson boys, Andrew, had caused some concern to his parents as a child as he seemed to never make any attempt to speak. His mother was deeply concerned that he might have some serious disability that meant he would never be able to talk. Then one day, when he was three years old and walking out with his mother, they were passing a row of agricultural machines of the type in use at that time. Something caught his eye and he stopped and looked at it intently. Suddenly he said quite clearly and correctly, "Harrow." So he had not only spoken, but had put two syllables together. After that his progress was rapid.

He was attracted to the family seafaring tradition and joined his first ship at Leith in 1919. Later he emigrated to Australia. During most of the Second World War he served on the *Matthew Flinders* which was on duty mainly in the Darwin and New Guinea area, and sometimes went as far north as Borneo.

After the war he served for many years as third mate on the *Abel Tasman*, running between Australia and New Zealand, and was said to have been very popular because of his ready wit. He was also skilled in woodwork and found time to make a fiddle which he gave to his brother, Hughie. He retired in 1963 and settled with his Australian-born wife, Esther, at their home, Da Noost, on the Woronora River. Later that year they made the long trip to Shetland to visit his surviving relatives.

When the youngest boy, Hughie, was very young his elder brothers were surprised and somewhat baffled by a rattling noise he made when he ran. Only when he turned out his pockets and they saw the mixture of old nails, washers, nuts and bolts, and other metallic oddments carried by boys of that age, was the mystery solved.

And if any of Hughie's family became concerned that his early breach of the law (taking Bobby Hugh's car for a run when he was 12) might lead to a life of crime, they worried needlessly. Following the family tradition he joined the merchant navy and was boatswain on the SS *Glenfarg* when she was torpedoed and sunk by gunfire on 4th October 1939. He helped to remove the ship's compass to take with himself and the rest of the crew when they were forced to take to the boats.

After retiring from the sea because of health problems, he trained as a piano tuner. During the school summer holidays he was in constant employment maintaining the pianos which were then a common fitment in many schools. He bought a vintage motorbike which he adapted to carry all his piano tuning equipment. The bike could be easily carried on the small motorboats which linked the islands together so he was able to carry on his work throughout Shetland. When he bought it it still had its old acetylene lighting and other obsolete equipment. Hughie removed all this and replaced it with modern devices, but retained it in case he might at some time want to rebuild it as a vintage motorcycle. Sadly, he never got around to it. He later served as a councillor on Shetland Islands Council and remained completely respectable all the rest of his life.

George, who was in the merchant navy, served as craneman/AB on MV *Prittlewell* at Scapa Flow. Later, he obtained a job as resident telephone linesman for Yell and Unst. He was supplied with two little green vans, once a common sight on all the roads in Britain. One van he used in Yell, and because he was also responsible for the phones in Unst a similar van was garaged there, which removed the need to rely on taxis. To reach Unst he had to cross the sometimes rather stormy Bluemull Sound, with a decidedly awkward pier at the Belmont side, but once across the sound a short walk from Belmont took him to where the second van was garaged and it was then easy to drive to wherever he was needed.

He was often troubled by heavy snowfalls, which were far more common in those days than they are today. One wintry Saturday afternoon in Yell he set out with a man called John Coghill to drive to Sellafirth on some errand or other. The weather was bad and at one point they thought of turning back, but decided to carry on. On the way back, however, it became much worse – a raging blizzard – and when they were almost at the top of Basta Hill the van became stuck fast in a snowdrift. At first they thought to walk home, but this would have been very dangerous, so they were greatly relieved when Dr Peterson's Land Rover came up behind them. This was the same Dr Peterson and the same Land Rover which was used to pull Willie back onto the road at Sellafirth on a different occasion. That time they had tied a rope from the Land Rover to the Film Guild van, but this time, perhaps because the snow was just too deep, they decided to leave the van to be recovered later and climbed aboard the Land Rover. Dr Peterson lived in North-a-Voe so he dropped off John Coghill at Camb and took George to his home in Seafield, where he spent the night before being rescued next morning by the snowplough. George went on to complete an amazing 23 years as linesman for Yell and Unst.

Henry, the third oldest brother, had, after many years as a ship's captain with the Sheaf Line, retired from the sea before the war and was living in Scatlands, West Sandwick with his parents and adopted sister Clara. When hostilities broke out he was told officially that either he or Clara would have to become involved in war work. One of them could remain at home to help with the croft. Henry thought that Clara would be more useful in croft work than he would so he returned to the sea once more. This was rather unfortunate as Clara was interested in nursing and would have been keen to train for that profession. But the survival of the croft had to take priority.

It seems likely that Henry served for a time on HMS *Lifeline*, an Admiralty salvage vessel. When he had leave he would come back to Shetland on one of the ships that ran regularly between Lerwick and Aberdeen. On his way to Yell he always visited Willie and his family who were at that time living in a flat in Bellevue House, at the top of Knab Road. They knew roughly when he would be coming and Kari always kept watch for him. When she saw him appear at the foot of Knab Road she would walk down to meet him and then accompany him up the road to Bellevue. There was a naval base at the top of the road so they often met naval ratings on the way. When this happened the navy men always saluted Henry, as he was an officer in uniform. The reflected glory of this made Kari feel tremendously important for days afterwards.

Henry also had a second career. After retiring from his distinguished career as a Master Mariner he taught navigation and seamanship in the local schools for many years.

The Williamson family was always very close and on one occasion it had been decided that the whole family was to attend communion service at the church. There were the six boys and three girls, plus their father and mother. All the boys rode motorcycles but their father, Willie Snr, didn't, so he would have to be taken on a pillion like the girls. On the occasion of the church visit one of his sons would have to take him as a pillion passenger.

Henry was chosen to perform this task. With hindsight, I think that this could have been better organised. Henry had been a mischievous boy but by this time he was well on his way to becoming a dedicated, professional seaman. His ambition was to pass his exams and qualify as Master Mariner and be captain of a ship, which he eventually achieved. Because of this he was often away from home for long periods and, as a result, he was probably less experienced in motorcycling than his brothers. His cycle was one of the strange looking types which had very long handlebars stretching back over the tank, like the handles of a wheelbarrow.

There is a certain amount of skill involved in being a pillion passenger and when they started off it soon became obvious that Willie Snr, probably again because of lack of experience, did not possess much of it. Single track roads in Yell at that time were less than two metres wide so there was little room for manoeuvre. Most of them also had deep ditches at both sides so they were quite unforgiving of mistakes. Henry and his father were soon in trouble, swinging wildly from one side of the road to the other with Henry trying desperately to steady the machine and take a straight course, a job made more difficult, and unintentionally comical, by the long, unwieldy handlebars. The whole scene became wildly hilarious, resembling a chase scene from a *Keystone Kops* movie.

However, the future Captain Henry Williamson was not a man to give up easily. Eventually he managed to regain some sort of control and, while still continuing his erratic progress, he finally brought his father safely to the church in time to meet up with the rest of the group and go to the service together.

No doubt they were all relieved at this point, but for Willie Jnr his troubles were just starting. He had had a grandstand view of the journey to church and the scenes he had witnessed had already become engraved on his memory and now came unbidden back to him. The hallowed atmosphere of the church made things worse. He had been so amused that at one point he had been hard pressed not to burst into laughter. This would not have mattered too much on the open road but in the solemn atmosphere of the church, in those days, it would have been unthinkable. It is no reflection on the minister, who no doubt delivered a good and inspiring sermon, but on that day at least one member of his congregation was heartily relieved when he pronounced the final "Amen," and brought the proceedings to a close.

Epilogue

Even many years after his retirement Willie's reputation still followed him. On one occasion he experienced something reminiscent of a Sherlock Holmes story. He was walking a short distance in the dark on the Mid Yell road when a motorcycle with a pillion passenger drove slowly past and stopped a short distance down the road. The driver raced the engine up before stopping it. This was a common practice at that time, the theory being that this might cause any unburned fuel to be retained in the combustion chamber, which would make it easier to re-start.

When the engine had stopped the passenger asked the driver, "Do you think that does any good?"

"I don't know," replied the driver, "a lot of people do it."

"Well," said the passenger, "Willie Williamson of North-a-Voe thought that it did no good at all."

He was perfectly correct. Rightly or wrongly, that had always been Willie's opinion.

* 9 7 8 1 9 1 0 9 9 7 5 5 0 *
BV - #0025 - 120324 - C0 - 210/148/5 - PB - 9781910997550 - Gloss Lamination